Hinck

Business Class

Wirtschaftsenglisch für kaufmännische Berufe

Merkur
Verlag Rinteln

Wirtschaftswissenschaftliche Bücherei für Schule und Praxis
Begründet von Handelsschul-Direktor Dipl.-Hdl. Friedrich Hutkap †

Verfasser:

Michael Hinck

* * * * *

5. Auflage 2022

Gesamtherstellung:
Merkur Verlag Rinteln Hutkap GmbH & Co. KG, 31735 Rinteln

E-Mail: info@merkur-verlag.de
lehrer-service@merkur-verlag.de
Internet: www.merkur-verlag.de

Merkur-Nr. 0855-05
ISBN 978-3-8120-0855-6

Vorwort

Aufgrund des neuartigen handlungsorientierten Konzeptes und modularen Aufbaus ist dieses umfassende und universell einsetzbare Praxisbuch sowohl für die kaufmännische Ausbildung in der Berufsschule als auch für vollzeitschulische Bildungsgänge, die Fachschule sowie Fort- und Weiterbildungen im Rahmen der berufsbegleitenden Erwachsenenbildung geeignet.

Es enthält zahlreiche unterschiedliche Aufgabentypen und Anwendungen zu betriebswirtschaftlichen Sachverhalten sowie abwechslungsreiche Übungen für die englischsprachige Geschäfts- und Handelskorrespondenz, vom Angebot bis zur Zahlungsaufforderung. Zudem werden die Erstellung und Gestaltung wichtiger unternehmensinterner Dokumente wie Memos, Protokolle und Berichte behandelt.

- Das Lehr- und Arbeitswerk vermittelt berufsbezogenes Englisch und aktive kommunikative Fähigkeiten für den Geschäftsalltag anhand realistischer und praxisorientierter Handlungssituationen aus dem Berufsalltag.
- Der Fokus liegt auf der Förderung der Kommunikationskompetenz und dem fächerübergreifenden Wissens- und Fremdsprachenerwerb mit hoher Aktivierung der Lernenden.
- Die Lernenden trainieren anwendungsorientiert mit zahlreichen praxisnahen und handlungsorientierten Aufgabenstellungen den speziellen Wortschatz für die schriftliche Kommunikation in der Geschäftswelt.
- Der modulare Aufbau und das handlungsorientierte Konzept erlauben den Einstieg auch in fortgeschrittene Kapitel und können passgenau nach Bedarf und dem zur Verfügung stehenden Zeitkontingent ausgewählt und bearbeitet werden.
- Die Lernenden haben ein kompaktes, integriertes Lern- und Arbeitswerk, sodass keinerlei zusätzliche Kopien erforderlich sind und die Teilnehmer ihr Material stets zur Hand haben, selbst wenn einmal eine Lektion oder Unterrichtseinheit versäumt wurde.
- Praktisches Layout auf Doppelseiten im Kapitel Business Correspondence mit Key Vocabulary, Key Phrases und Sample Letters auf der einen Seite und Handlungssituationen und Aufgaben auf der anderen Seite erleichtern die Erarbeitung.
- Der Anhang dient als nützliches Nachschlagewerk mit alphabetischen Wortlisten, Abkürzungen und einer Übersicht der unregelmäßigen Verben.

Für die vorliegende **fünfte Auflage** wurde das Lehr- und Arbeitsbuch um zahlreiche Übungen zur Erweiterung des Wortschatzes ergänzt. Im Fokus stehen dabei häufig verwendete Phrasal Verbs aus der betrieblichen Praxis des Berufsalltags, welche für das Verständnis essenziell sind und zudem den Ausdruck verbessern.

Frühjahr 2022

Michael Hinck

Inhaltsverzeichnis

Unit 1: Die eigene Rolle im Betrieb mitgestalten und den Betrieb präsentieren

Unit 2: Büroprozesse gestalten und Arbeitsvorgänge organisieren

Unit 3: Aufträge bearbeiten

Unit 4: Kunden akquirieren und binden

Unit 5: Gesprächssituationen bewältigen

UNIT 6: PERSONALWIRTSCHAFTLICHE AUFGABEN WAHRNEHMEN

UNIT 7: VERANSTALTUNGEN UND GESCHÄFTSREISEN ORGANISIEREN

Unit 1: Die eigene Rolle im Betrieb mitgestalten und den Betrieb präsentieren

1 Talking about your work and your company

Being part of today's business world requires thorough communication. Good conversation skills are vital to be successful in business. When dealing with customers and business associates always be polite and friendly. All things being equal, people prefer to do business with friends. All things being unequal, people still prefer to do business with friends.

You will often encounter businessmen and clients from abroad. When conducting business with English speaking persons, you usually introduce yourself using your first and last name. However, it is common to be addressed only by one's first name, e.g. "Hello Mr Stevens. I am Ann Miller, but please call me Ann".

After you have been introduced, the opportunity for conversation arises. It is essential that you are able to talk about your work and your company. Prepare and practise the following themes:

- Introduce yourself and give details about your education and professional training.
- Describe the company you work for, what your company does and where it is located.
- Give an example of a specific product or service your company provides. Highlight its advantages or characteristics and explain how customers or other companies benefit from your company's goods and services.
- Explain what you do for your company, in which department you work and what your position is.

2 Useful phrases for describing your company and its products

Talking about…

✔ **your company's history**

Our company was founded in 1987.
It was established in…

✔ **your company's products and services**

We produce/manufacture/make/supply…
Our company provides/offers …
We are developing …
We are conducting research on …
We (also) operate in the field of …

✔ **your company's structure**

Our company is based in…
Our head office is located in Brussels, Belgium.
Our headquarters is located in the city centre of…
Our production facilities/factories/laboratories are…
We have subsidiaries in the UK and in Germany.
We have three (main) divisions, which are…
We cooperate with…/do business with…
Our company has more than 3,000 employees.
We have a workforce of more than 3,000 people.
We are listed on the Frankfurt/London/New York Stock Exchange.

✔ **your company's performance**

We are the market leaders in the field of …
We are the largest manufacturer of …
in the world./in Europe./the UK.
We have expanded our operations to …
Our market share has grown by 36 %.
Our revenue is in excess of € 14 million.
Last month/quarter/year we achieved
a profit of more than $ 144,000/$ 4 million.
Our (main) customers are …

✔ **your responsibilities**

I came to [company's name] in 20.. [year].
I joined the company in 20.. [year].
I have been with [company's name] …
I have worked at the company …
I have worked in the marketing department … for more than 3 years./… for almost 5 years. … since March [month]/… since 20.. [year].
I work as …/I'm the …
I am responsible for …/I deal with …
I am in charge of …/I take care of …
I head up/run the IT department.
I make sure …/I ensure …
I coordinate/organize/manage …
My role is to …/My job involves …
My responsibilities are …
I report to the Chief Marketing Manager.

Exercise – Different lines of business

A2

Match the expressions listed below to the corresponding items.

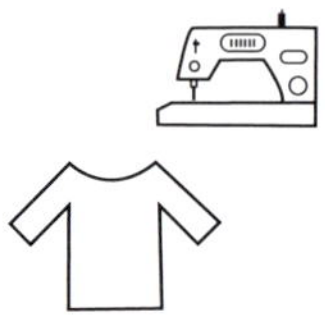
(a) ....

(b) ....

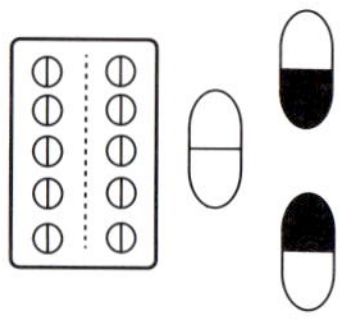
(c) ....

(d) ....

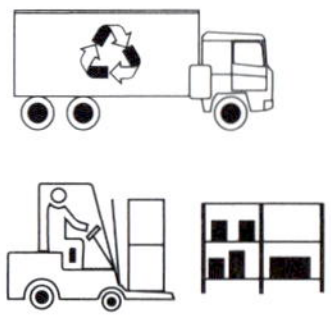
(e) ....

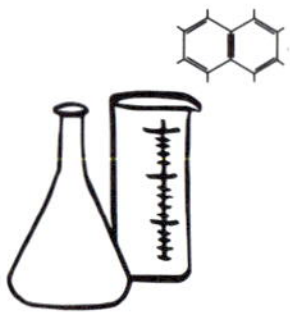
(f) ....

(g) ....

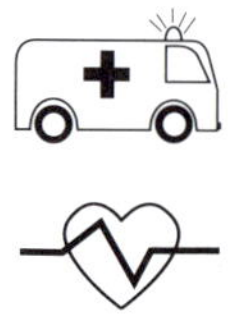
(h) ....

(i) ....

(j) ....

(k) ....

(l) ....

(m) ....

(n) ....

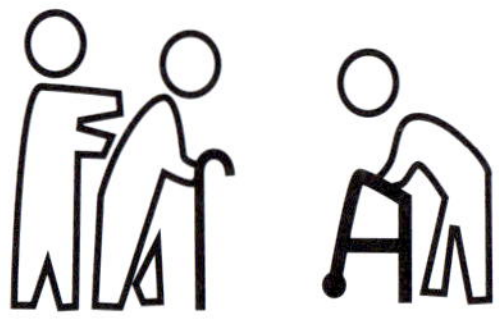
(o) ....

(p) ....

Accounting | Aerospace and Aviation | Agriculture | Automotive Technology | Banking | Chemistry, Laboratory and Research | Childcare Services | Computing and Information Technology | Construction and Building | Education | Electronics | Engineering | Environmental Technology | Event Management | Fashion, Apparel and Textiles | Food Industry | Geriatric Care and Nursing | Human Resources/ Personnel Management | Industry/ Manufacturing | Law/ Legal Affairs | Marketing/ Sales | Media and Entertainment Industry | Medical and Healthcare Services | Pharmaceutics and Pharmacology | Postal Services | Publication and Journalism | Retail | Secretarial Services and Administration | Taxation | Telecommunications | Tourism and Travel | Warehousing / Storage, Transport and Logistics

Exercise – Visualizing the organizational structure (1)

A2

Background

You work in the personnel department and are responsible for supervising new apprentices and trainees. For an upcoming seminar you would like to illustrate the business-to-customer relationship and a typical organizational structure.

Assignment

Match the expressions listed below to the corresponding items.

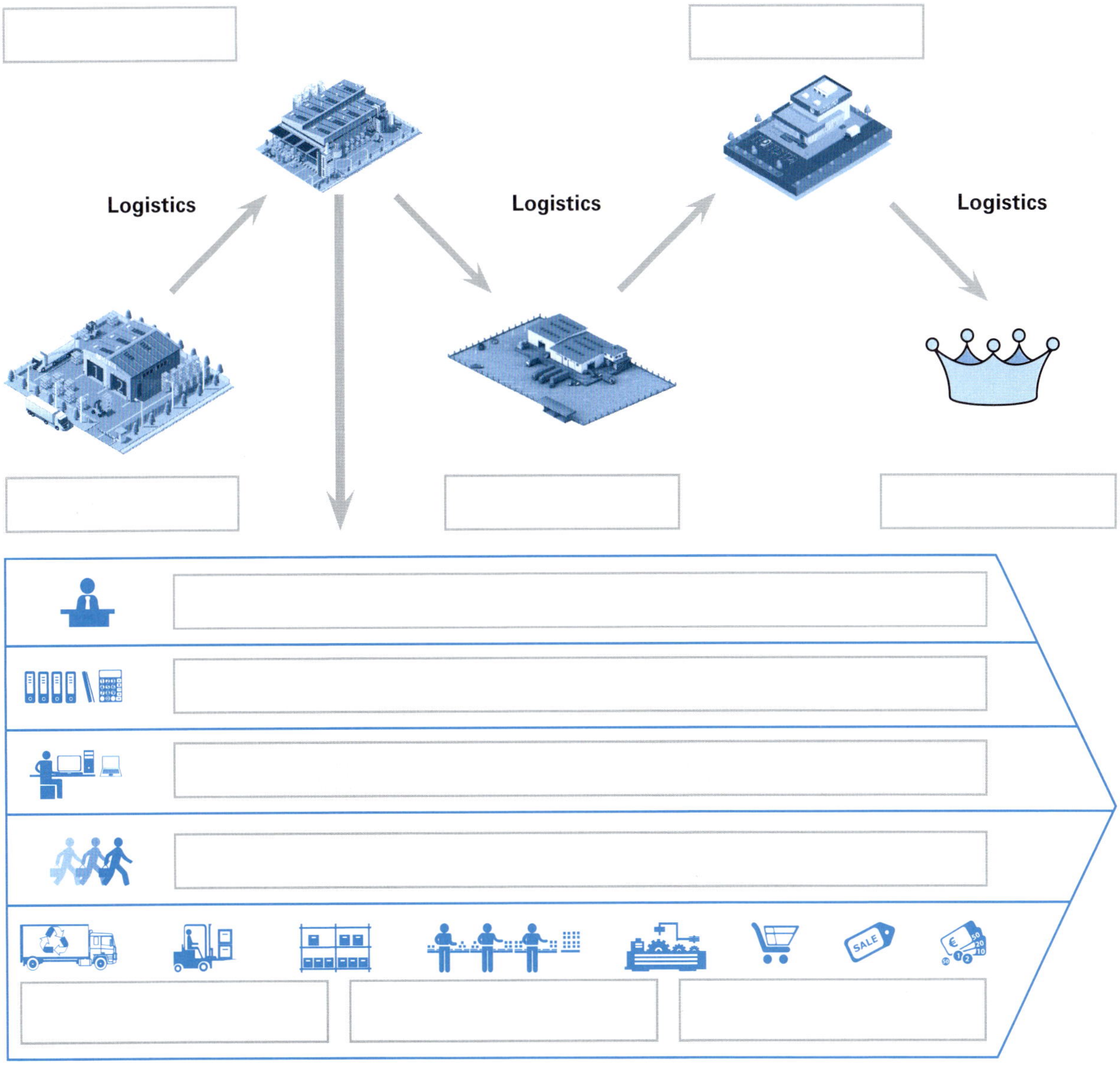

Accounting/Bookkeeping	Marketing/Sales
Customer	Procurement/Purchasing
Human Resources/Personnel	Production/Manufacturing
Information Technology (IT)	Retailer
Managing Director/President / CEO	Supplier
Manufacturer	Wholesaler

Exercise – Visualizing the organizational structure (2)

A2

Background

It is your first day on the job and you are about to start in the Public Relations Department. You are talking to Carol Porter, who is describing the structure of the department:

"You will join Janet Baker's team. Janet is the PR & Sponsoring Manager. She will be able to help and support you in the upcoming weeks. Her superior is Eric White, the Head of Communications. You met him earlier on in his office. Janet reports to him; as do the Advertising Manager Robert Blake and Thomas Anderson, the Social Media Manager. That's Thomas over there at the photocopier. You're going to have three colleagues in PR: Samuel Norton, Steven Robbins and Jane Miller, who brought the coffee a few minutes ago. John Dixon is the Head of Market Research. He's not in the office today, but you'll meet him tomorrow. And then there is Steve Gomez, our third department head besides John and Eric. Steve is responsible for Sales and Distribution. At the top of the entire Marketing Department is Jack Carter, our Marketing Director, who we're going to see now. Jack reports directly to his boss at the top of the company, the Managing Director, Shane Walsh. Oh and I'm Jack's Personal Assistant, so if you would like to contact him and he's too busy, just leave it with me and I'll take care of it."

Assignment

Complete the organizational chart of the marketing department.

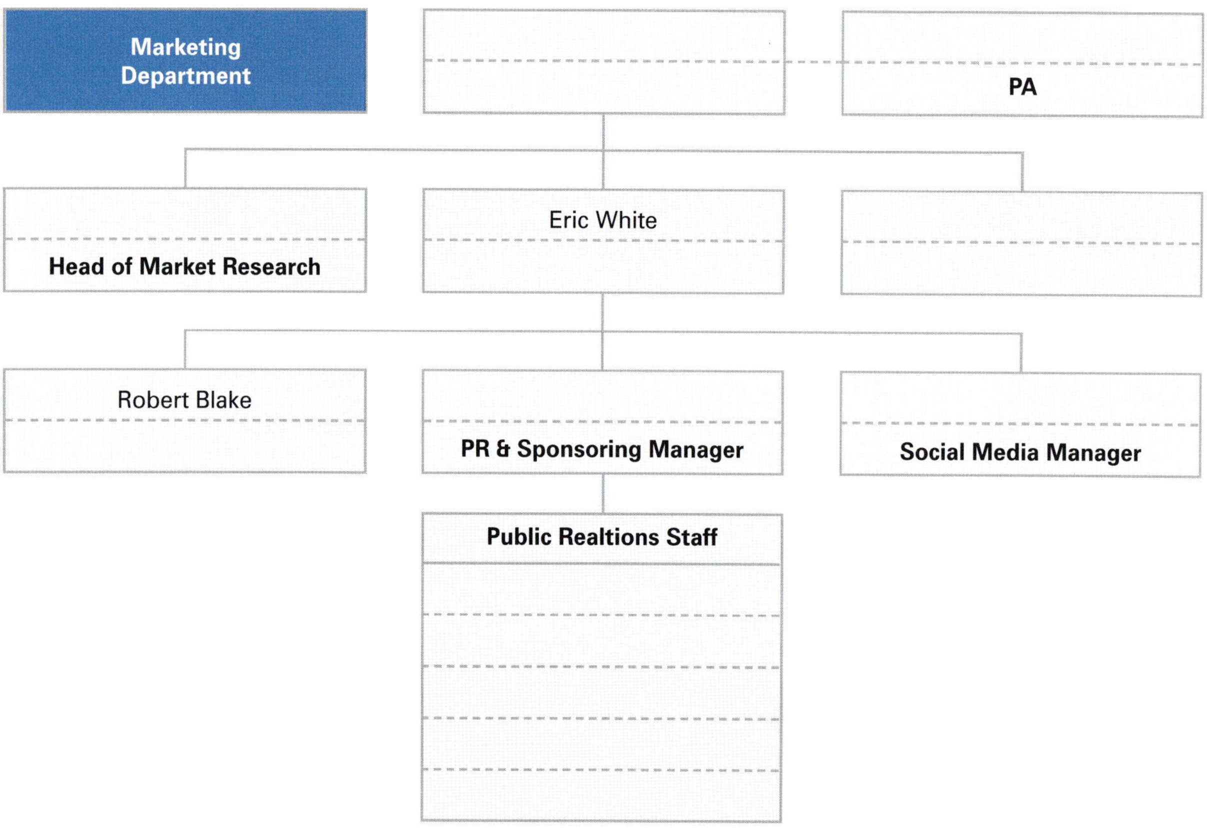

Unit 2: Büroprozesse gestalten und Arbeitsvorgänge organisieren

1 Time Management

Time is the currency of the 21st century. It is indispensable and the most valuable factor in production. All work requires time. Even thinking about work before you begin working requires time. Time is perishable. It cannot be saved or substituted. It can only be reallocated.

There is a fundamental law, which you have to accept: There is never enough time to do everything, but there is always enough time to do the most important things.

Make decisions quickly. 80 % of all decisions can be made the moment they come up. Don't delay or procrastinate on them. Make decisions as often as possible. Decisiveness is developed through practise and repetition. You will get better at making decisions and save yourself a lot of time.

Decide to make time management your core skill. Complete all "quick jobs" as soon as they come up. Anything that will take you less than two minutes is usually something that should be done immediately. Answer emails and return telephone calls instantly – but be brief! Whenever possible and appropriate, make a phone call instead of writing an email or letter.

Tidy up and keep one task on your desk at a time. Plan every day in advance. The 10 % time you spend planning your activities before you begin will save you as much as 90 % of the time necessary to complete those activities once you've started working. Always think on paper and always work from a list. According to time management experts, working from a list will increase your productivity by 25 %. By systematically prioritising your tasks you can even double your productivity!

Learn to say no and don't set or accept tight deadlines. It is not true that you work best under pressure. This is only a justification for poor time management. You simply experience more stress and make more unnecessary and costly mistakes. You should rather "underpromise" and "overdeliver". Discipline yourself to get the job done in advance, do it properly and give it "your own spin".

Besides, it is often unnecessary to be a perfectionist. Apply the 80/20 rule, (also known as the "Pareto Principle"), and focus on the most valuable top 20 % of activities that produce 80 % of your results. Set yourself a deadline at which point you will decide to accept that the work you've done so far is "thorough enough". Understand that it won't necessarily turn out to be twice as valuable if you invest 200 % of your time and energy.

Practise "single-handling" with key tasks. This technique alone will instantly boost your productivity by 50 % or more. First, make a list of everything you have to do. Then select the most important item on your list; the most valuable use of your time. Start work on that most important task and discipline yourself to stay at it until it's 100 % complete. If you start a task and then put it aside and keep coming back to it later and starting again, the time required to perform that task often increases by 500 %. On the other hand, if you pick a task and discipline yourself to stay at it until it's done, you can decrease the amount of time it takes to do that task by as much as 80 %.

Finally, when you work, you work. Don't socialise, drink coffee or check your private emails while you are working. Work all the time you work! And always ask: "What is the most valuable use of my time right now?"

Time management is not just a peripheral or secondary skill. It is actually the core skill upon which everything else is based. Time management is not a planet which is revolving around the sun. Time management is the sun and everything else you do has to be seen as the planets. The minutes and hours of each day are the fundamental building blocks of your personal and business success.

Answer the following questions using complete sentences.

A2

(1) Why is it not advisable to work under pressure?

____

(2) Explain the concept of "single handling".

____

(3) What is meant by the "Pareto Principle"?

____

____

Exercise – Scheduling appointments

A2

Background

You work as the Personal Assistant to the Managing Director of a large multinational company. One of your tasks is to keep his monthly diary up to date.

He has left you the following notes about his appointments (engagements) for the coming month:

- I'm out of office every Thursday (except 22nd) for the Regional Sales Meeting
- two-day guided tour of our new plant in Brussels on the last weekend
- Logistics Committee meets weekly on Monday afternoon
- 2nd and 4th Tuesday Marketing Review Meetings
- Wednesdays Team Briefings & Coaching (except week 3)
- visit from Mr Hattori Matsumoto, Japanese company delegate, on the second weekend
- Design Awards Exhibition in Cologne, starts on 21st (three days in total)
- Steering Group Meeting on the last Friday of the month
- 1st and 3rd Saturday of each month business lunch at The Brandon
- visit to IT Tech Trade Fair in Geneva, Friday before the Design Awards Exhibition
- 1st two Fridays – Planning Review Meetings
- Directors' Video Conference – Tuesday after the first business lunch
- 1st Monday morning of each month – Monthly Board Meeting
- 2nd Monday morning of each month – Local Authority Meeting
- last Monday morning of each month – Project Team Meeting

Assignment

Use the information above to complete your boss's diary on the next page:

Date	Weekday	Appointment
1st	Thursday	
2nd	Friday	
3rd	Saturday	
4th	Sunday	
5th	Monday	
6th	Tuesday	
7th	Wednesday	
8th	Thursday	
9th	Friday	
10th	Saturday	
11th	Sunday	
12th	Monday	
13th	Tuesday	
14th	Wednesday	
15th	Thursday	
16th	Friday	
17th	Saturday	
18th	Sunday	
19th	Monday	
20th	Tuesday	
21st	Wednesday	
22nd	Thursday	
23rd	Friday	
24th	Saturday	
25th	Sunday	
26th	Monday	
27th	Tuesday	
28th	Wednesday	
29th	Thursday	
30th	Friday	

2 Setting Priorities with the Eisenhower Matrix

"What is important is seldom urgent and what is urgent is seldom important."

– Dwight D. Eisenhower, former US Army general and the 34th President of the United States

The Eisenhower Matrix is a framework used for dividing tasks/activities into four categories, so-called quadrants:
(1) important and urgent,
(2) important, but not urgent,
(3) not important, but urgent and
(4) not important and not urgent.

Important and urgent: These are unplanned and unwanted emergencies, which have to be addressed immediately: machinery breakdowns, troubleshooting, deadlines and so forth. Solve these problems immediately. Then ask yourself what you can do avoid these crises in the future. If possible, take measures or make preparations to ensure that these emergencies don't happen again. Your best option is to **DO IT IMMEDIATELY**

Important, but not urgent: These are important long-term activities, like planning and preparation. It is not necessary to perform these tasks immediately, but neglecting these important and necessary responsibilities will make these matters urgent in the future and will lead to new crises and emergencies. These are the most important tasks to focus on, as they are important, yet not urgent. Your best bet is to **PLAN & SCHEDULE** these tasks.

Not important, but urgent: These issues are interruptions and distractions, which are not important to your business goals, but have to be dealt with, like answering unnecessary emails, incoming phone calls, interrupting colleagues or minor complaints from customers. Try to delegate or avoid these as much as possible. Once you've been interrupted, handle them as fast as possible. Your best strategy is to **DELEGATE, MINIMIZE & AVOID** these items.

Neither urgent nor important: These tasks are completely useless and should be eliminated. These include unnecessary paperwork, surfing the internet aimlessly, non-work related social-media activities, checking emails every couple of minutes or other time wasters. **ELIMINATE** these activities from the workplace altogether.

Exercise – Using the Eisenhower Matrix to prioritise tasks/activities

A2

Always ask yourself these two questions: **"Is it urgent?" & "Is it important?"**

- working on a long-term project
- junk mail
- learning a language
- overdue invoices
- helping someone with unnecessary paperwork
- building & maintaining professional relationships
- petty complaint from a small customer
- developing professional qualifications
- playing with your mobile phone
- phone call from your boss
- gossiping
- interrupting co-workers
- advertising calls from suppliers
- serious complaint from a large customer
- surfing the web without any real objective
- strategic plan, due in three months
- quarterly report, due today
- preparing an upcoming seminar
- Facebook
- reading newsletters
- unnecessary phone calls
- tidying up
- hospital emergencies
- looking after your health

Assign the items to the correct quadrant:

Exercise – Vocabulary Building – Basic Opposites

A2

Choose an appropriate opposite from the list below:

large	____________	huge	____________
new	____________	long	____________
late	____________	rich	____________
cheap	____________	high	____________
hard	____________	hot	____________
thin	____________	dry	____________
dark	____________	easy	____________
boring	____________	all	____________
clean	____________	slow	____________
quiet	____________	alike	____________
full	____________	wide	____________
dangerous	____________	seldom	____________
simple	____________	light	____________
always	____________	exact	____________
near	____________	true	____________
more	____________	strong	____________
broken	____________	odd	____________
allowed	____________	optional	____________

approximate	bright	cold	complex	different	difficult
dirty	early	empty	even	expensive	false
far	fast	intact	interesting	heavy	less
low	mandatory	narrow	never	noisy	nothing
often	old	poor	prohibited	safe	short
small	soft	thick	tiny	weak	wet

A2

Translate the following sentences into English using some of the opposites from the previous exercise.

(1) Dies ist eine **schwierige** Situation und wir benötigen so **schnell** wie möglich eine Entscheidung.

____

(2) Es ist **nie** zu **spät,** eine Alternative zu finden.

____

(3) Sogar eine **kleine** Änderung ist relativ **teuer.**

____

(4) Es ist **immer gefährlich,** sich auf eine **einfache** Lösung zu verlassen.

____

(5) Ein **winziger** Fehler kann ein **riesiges** Problem verursachen.

____

(6) Die Umsätze waren zu **niedrig** und die Kosten zu **hoch.**

____

(7) Das Modell ist **gleich,** aber die Artikelnummer ist **unterschiedlich.**

____

(8) Das Unternehmen bietet eine **breite** Produktpalette.

____

(9) In den Geschäftsräumen ist das Rauchen **verboten.**

____

(10) Die Teilnahme an der Sitzung ist **freiwillig.**

____

(11) Die Schätzung basiert auf **falschen** Informationen.

____

(12) Die benötigten Daten sind **selten** verfügbar.

____

(13) Dieser Wert ist eine **ungefähre** Zahl.

____

(14) Wie das Sprichwort sagt: „Wenn es nicht **kaputt** ist, repariere es nicht!".

____

(15) Die Verwendung von Sicherheitsgurten ist **vorgeschrieben.**

____

Exercise – Vocabulary Building – Phrasal Verbs with COME

B1 B2

Phrasal verbs are a combination of a verb and a preposition or an adverb. They are an essential part of the English language and are commonly used by native speakers. Phrasal verbs are extremely important for fluency when learning English and will greatly improve your understanding and vocabulary skills to communicate effectively. Note that each phrasal verb can have multiple different meanings.

Choose the matching preposition for each phrasal verb:

come	__________	= break, separate	come	__________	= contract or get an illness
come	__________	= make progress	come	__________	= change one's opinion
come	__________	= invent, think of, create, offer	come	__________	= happen, occur
come	__________	= keep one's promise, succeed	come	__________	= find something by accident
come	__________	= amount to, boil down to	come	__________	= obtain, get

across | along | apart | around | by

down to | down with | through | up | up with

Fill in the appropriate phrasal verb for each sentence. Remember to adapt the tense of the verb when necessary.

(1) Call me back asap. Something's ____________________.

(2) When I went through the files, I ____________________ the document you were looking for.

(3) Retail sales are ____________________ nicely.

(4) We were concerned she wouldn't do it, but she ____________________.

(5) It all ____________________ money in the end.

(6) The head of department doesn't agree, but don't worry. He'll ________________ eventually.

(7) When I picked up the folder, it ____________________ in my hands.

(8) Reliable employees are rather hard to ____________________.

(9) Many people ____________________ with the flu last winter.

(10) We have to ____________________ a solution to this urgent problem.

Exercise – Vocabulary Building – Phrasal Verbs with GO

B1 B2

Phrasal verbs are a combination of a verb and a preposition or an adverb. They are an essential part of the English language and are commonly used by native speakers. Phrasal verbs are extremely important for fluency when learning English and will greatly improve your understanding and vocabulary skills to communicate effectively. Note that each phrasal verb can have multiple different meanings.

Choose the matching preposition for each phrasal verb:

go ____________	= continue, proceed	go ____________	= examine, scrutinize, analyze
go ____________	= accept, agree, participate, cooperate	go ____________	= violate, breach, = oppose
go ____________	= get involved in, investigate, explore	go ____________	= be denied, be deprived of
go ____________	= pursue an object or goal, try, attempt	go ____________	= start to do something
go ____________	= explode, fire, begin making noise	go ____________	= dealing with a situation in a particular way

about | after | against | ahead | along with

into | off | on | over | without

Fill in the correct phrasal verb for each sentence. Remember to adapt the tense of the verb when necessary.

(1) There are no copies left, so I'm afraid you'll just have to ____________________.

(2) We need to ____________________ the reports to make sure we haven't missed anything.

(3) The alarm will ____________________ at six o'clock.

(4) I don't want to ____________________ the details now.

(5) Please ____________________ with what you're doing and don't let us interrupt you.

(6) Alright. I will ____________________ you on that matter.

(7) We've received permission to ____________________ with the project.

(8) What you're asking me to do ____________________ everything I believe in.

(9) The company is ____________________ the software market in Austria.

(10) Management thinks we should ____________________ this issue quite differently.

3 Organizing Meetings and Conferences

Meetings and conferences are similar in that people get together to discuss a particular subject. The main difference lies in the scale of the event. Usually, a meeting involves fewer people and is often conducted in-house, while conferences are held at outside venues such as conference rooms in hotels or training centres, which are specifically designed to hold more attendees.

Large conferencences are often referred to as conventions and are even larger get-togethers of professionals from many different companies.

Meetings are generally over in a matter of hours, can be held at a short notice and are sometimes rather casual. Conferences or conventions are more formal affairs which can last several days. They therefore require long-term planning, invitations, travel arrangements and accommodation for the participants, e.g. company delegates, speakers.

When planning a meeting or conference, a variety of points have to be considered:

You should have an extensive knowledge of your manager's business associates and should be aware of how to contact them. You should consider where the meeting will take place and how long it will last.

Contact people as early as possible in advance and offer alternative dates to cover any eventualities that may arise. Having contacted the participants, it is vital to seek confirmation and make any necessary adjustments to the schedule.

Take into consideration that external visitors will need extra time to travel to your offices or conference venues. Schedule meetings appropriately. Approach internal staff as soon as you are aware of any meeting involving them. This allows them time to adjust their schedules. It is a advisable to be familiar with the schedules of the firm's key people.

In the event of someone not being able to attend, find out whether other methods may be employed, like telephone-, web-, or video-conferencing.

Contact the appropriate departments involved for any relevant material required for the meeting, such as files, reports, figures, data and so on. Ensure that any equipment needed is available at the venue, e.g. notebook, projector, flipchart and the like. Remember to ensure that suitable refreshments are provided.

Your arrangements must be convenient to your superior as his/her schedule is your main priority.

An agenda for the meeting, stating who is attending and what topics are to be addressed will also be required. The agenda should be sent out to all participants in advance of the event.

Checklists – Organizing Meetings

Before calling a meeting, ask yourself the following questions:

- ✓ Does the matter require support, consensus or discussion?
- ✓ Could the issue be handled without a meeting?
- ✓ Could it be managed with an email or a memo?

Decide why the meeting is being held:

- ✓ decision-making
- ✓ persuasion
- ✓ information exchange
- ✓ brainstorming
- ✓ motivation
- ✓ delegation

Before calling a meeting, consider the following hints for organizing and conducting meetings:

- ✓ Start and stop on time.
- ✓ Consider starting at odd times – for example 8:10 or 9:20. This tends to increase punctuality.
- ✓ Try to avoid typical one-hour meetings. Ask yourself: Would thirty/forty/fifty minutes do?
- ✓ Remember to bring extra copies of the agenda.
- ✓ Always stick to the agenda and distribute the time efficiently.
- ✓ Only one person should speak at a time.
- ✓ Don't let one or two people dominate the discussion.
- ✓ Stop side conversations by saying kindly: "I'd appreciate your input. Is there something you're saying that we need to know?"

A2

Mark whether the following statements are true or false.

		true	false
(1)	The majority of meetings doesn't require any planning or preparation.	☐	☐
(2)	Participants should be contacted well in advance.	☐	☐
(3)	Meetings are mainly conducted for information exchange.	☐	☐
(4)	It is not always necessary to use an agenda.	☐	☐
(5)	It is crucial to take your superior's timetable into consideration.	☐	☐
(5)	Most conferences and conventions are held in-house.	☐	☐
(6)	Meetings can have a variety of different objectives and purposes.	☐	☐
(7)	The time and location of a meeting are all you have to consider.	☐	☐
(8)	Conferences and conventions usually have more participants than meetings.	☐	☐
(9)	Departments concerned are best contacted at short notice.	☐	☐
(10)	You should always go for standard one-hour or two-hour meetings.	☐	☐
(11)	People who work in your own company are usually more flexible.	☐	☐
(12)	It is important to confirm that the invitation or message has been received.	☐	☐
(13)	It is advisable to let one or two participants dominate the discussion.	☐	☐

A2

Give an appropriate synonym from the text for each of the following words:

attendees	______	place	______
topic	______	informal	______
certain	______	ways/means	______
divisions/units	______	timetable	______
appropriate	______	preparations	______
necessary	______	important	______
especially	______	friends/contacts	______
changes	______	normally	______
company	______	wide/broad	______

Exercise – Vocabulary Building – Proverbs

B1

Learning proverbs, sayings and idioms is an excellent way to improve your fluency. Study the following proverbs and use them regularly in conversation and writing. It will enrich your vocabulary, enhance your comprehension and you will be able to communicate easily and fluently with native speakers in no time.

Complete the proverbs by matching the corresponding parts:

- Practice
- No pain
- A thing begun
- Don't judge a book
- Every cloud
- Ignorance
- Don't put the cart
- Don't count your chickens
- Let sleeping dogs
- Better safe
- Look
- It is not over
- Make hay
- Better late
- All that glitters
- When in Rome
- You can't have your cake
- It's no use
- You can't make an omelette
- You can't unscramble
- Don't put all your eggs
- If you can't beat them
- If it isn't broken
- Lightning never strikes
- A stitch in time
- All's well

- and eat it.
- before the horse.
- before they hatch.
- before you leap.
- by its cover.
- crying over spilt milk.
- do as the Romans do.
- don't fix it.
- has a silver lining.
- is bliss.
- is half done.
- is not gold.
- in one basket.
- join them.
- lie.
- makes perfect.
- no gain.
- than never.
- than sorry.
- that ends well.
- the same place twice.
- until it's over.
- saves nine.
- scrambled eggs.
- while the sun shines.
- without breaking eggs.

B1

Read these definitions and choose the appropriate proverbs from the previous exercise.

(1) No matter how bad a situation might seem, there is always some positive aspect to it.

____

(2) Do not concentrate all efforts and resources in only one venture, as you could lose everything.

____

(3) Avoid interfering in a situation that is currently not causing any problems, but may well do so as a result of such interference.

____

(4) It is advisable to respect and follow the custom of the native people while visiting their country.

____

(5) If something is working adequately well, leave it alone and don't mess with it.

____

(6) Don't make plans based on a good thing happening, before it has actually happened.

____

(7) A person, who doesn't know about a problem, doesn't worry about it.

____

(8) Don't be upset about a past mistake that cannot be undone.

____

(9) The outward appearance cannot be an indicator of someone's competence or something's value.

____

(10) Don't do things in the wrong order or sequence.

____

(11) The final outcome of a situation cannot be assumed until it reaches its end.

____

(12) Think carefully about the possible results or consequences before doing something.

____

(13) You can't enjoy both of two desirable but mutually exclusive alternatives.

____

(14) Take advantage of an opportunity while conditions are good.

____

(15) Don't wait too long to deal with a specific problem or you risk it getting much worse later on.

____

4 Writing Memos

In the age of the internet, it might seem old-fashioned to write a paper-based memo (memo is short for memorandum in singular or memoranda in plural) when you could send an email or text a short message instead.

There are, however, still many reasons for an employee to send a hardcopy memo to someone else. Memos are useful in situations where emails or text messages are not appropriate. Sometimes information needs to be delivered to a large number of employees to their physical mailboxes in the office, or an urgent message needs to get directly to the in-basket on someone's desk. Furthermore, certain matters require faxing documents to other companies or organizations, e.g. government offices, workshops or warehouses. Moreover, memos can be included or attached when sending packages or paper documents which require explanations, instructions or signatures. In these cases memos can be used as cover notes to explain what the receiver should do.

Memos are usually used for internal communication, e.g. writing to staff, department heads and so on. Typically, memos are used to inform others about new procedures or changes, to announce meetings or events, to communicate decisions or to make proposals.

A memo is usually fairly short (a few short paragraphs) and the language is more direct than in a letter. Focus on relevant information and leave out unnecessary details, but be polite. Say what you need to say in as few words as possible. Do not use a greeting or salutation. Instead, you should come straight to the point. It is not necessary to sign the memo, though sometimes the signature or the sender's name is included at the bottom. This may vary depending on the rules and regulations set by the company in which you work.

Layout of a memo

DRAGON COMPANY

Memo

To: All Staff
From: Eric Miller, IT Coordinator
Date: 11 March 20 ..
Subject: IT meeting on 25 March 20..

Please note that the IT meeting will take place in conference room No. 7 on 25 August 20 .. at 1400 hrs.

Attendance is mandatory, as you will receive new user IDs and passwords for network login and database access.

If you are unable to attend, please contact me immediately.

Thank you for your cooperation in this matter.

Eric Miller

Note: The signature is optional

Always follow the **KISS principle:**
KISS is an acronym for
Keep It Short and **Simple**

A suitable structure of a memo might be:

- **situation/problem**
- **solution/action**
- **closing**

Useful phrases for starting a memo:

Please note that ...
I wish to bring to your attention (that) ...
We have noticed (that) ...
I need/would like to inform/remind you about/of ...
You will probably have heard (that/about) ...
You are probably aware that/of ...
I am sure you all know that/about ...
It has come to our attention that ...
I am writing to let you know (that/about) ...

Use bullets to list information whenever possible.

Always remember to check spelling, grammar and punctuation.

Exercise – Calling a meeting

A2

Ihr Unternehmen plant die Eröffnung einer zweiten Filiale *(branch)* in einer anderen Stadt.

Schreiben Sie im Namen des Geschäftsführers *(Managing Director)* ein Memo an alle Abteilungsleiter *(Department Heads)* und laden Sie diese zu einem Meeting am 15. des nächsten Monats ein.

Das Meeting beginnt um 14:10 Uhr und wird voraussichtlich 1½ Stunden dauern. Es findet in Raum 19 im 3. Stock statt.

Bitten Sie die Teilnehmer darum, pünktlich zu erscheinen und den letzten Abteilungsbericht *(department report)* mitzubringen.

Falls jemand nicht teilnehmen kann, wird um eine Nachricht gebeten.

DRAGON COMPANY

Memo

To:

From:

Date:

Subject:

Exercise – Vocabulary Building – False Friends

A2

False friends are words in two languages that look or sound similar, but have a significantly different meaning in the other language.

Choose the correct translation from the list below:

ENGLISH	GERMAN	GERMAN	ENGLISH
actual	____________	aktuell	____________
to become	____________	bekommen	____________
chef	____________	Chef	____________
eventually	____________	eventuell	____________
quote	____________	Quote	____________
formula	____________	Formular	____________
fabric	____________	Fabrik	____________
concurrence	____________	Konkurrenz	____________
loan	____________	Lohn	____________
map	____________	Mappe	____________
meaning	____________	Meinung	____________
notice	____________	Notiz	____________
personal	____________	Personal	____________
prospect	____________	Prospekt	____________
process	____________	Prozess (Gericht)	____________
to spend	____________	spenden	____________
warehouse	____________	Warenhaus	____________
undertaker	____________	Unternehmer	____________

Ablauf/Verfahren/Vorgang · Angebot/Zitat · Aussicht/möglicher Neukunde · Bedeutung/Sinn · boss · brochure/leafleat · competition · current · Darlehen/Kredit · department store · eigentlich/tatsächlich · entrepreneur · factory · folder · form · Formel · Geld ausgeben/Zeit verbringen · Gewebe/Stoff · Hinweis/Aushang/Kündigung · Koch · Lagerhalle · Landkarte · Leichenbestatter · Mitwirkung/Gleichzeitigkeit · note · opinion · persönlich · personnel/staff · possibly/maybe · rate/share/proportion/quota · schließlich/letztendlich/irgendwann · to donate · to get · trial/lawsuit/legal action · wage · werden

A2

Translate the following sentences into English using some of the expressions from the previous exercise.

(1) Das **Prospekt** befindet sich in meiner **Mappe** auf dem Schreibtisch.

___

(2) Die **Meinung** unserer Kunden ist außerordentlich wichtig.

___

(3) Bitte hinterlassen Sie eine **Notiz** für die Sekretärin.

___

(4) Es ist immer gut, Geld zu **spenden.**

___

(5) Das neue **Warenhaus** wird zusätzliches **Personal** benötigen.

___

(6) Bitte schicken Sie uns Ihren **aktuellen** Katalog.

___

(7) Der **Chef** ist gerade in einer Besprechung.

___

(8) Die neue **Fabrik** wird die **Quote eventuell** erfüllen.

___

(9) Bitte füllen Sie das **Formular** aus.

___

(10) Die **Konkurrenz** bietet eine ausgezeichnete Produktpalette.

___

(11) Der **Lohn** wird am Ende des Monats überwiesen.

___

(12) Er ist ein kluger und fleißiger **Unternehmer.**

___

(13) Der **Prozess** wird nächsten Monat stattfinden.

___

(14) Wir benötigen das **tatsächliche Angebot.**

___

(15) Könnte ich einen Chickenburger **bekommen?**

___

Exercise – Vocabulary Building – Phrasal Verbs with LOOK

B1 B2

Phrasal verbs are a combination of a verb and a preposition or an adverb. They are an essential part of the English language and are commonly used by native speakers. Phrasal verbs are extremely important for fluency when learning English and will greatly improve your understanding and vocabulary skills to communicate effectively. Note that each phrasal verb can have multiple different meanings.

Choose the matching preposition for each phrasal verb:

look	__________	= think about s.th. in the past	look	__________	= inspect or search a place
look	__________	= regard s.o. as inferior	look	__________	= be vigilant and aware
look	__________	= search, seek	look	__________	= watch, protect, keep safe
look	__________	= consider or anticipate the future	look	__________	= investigate, explore, consider
look	__________	= obtain information about s.th. from a text source	look	__________	= feel excited about s.th. that is going to happen

after | ahead | back | down on | for
forward to | into | out | round/around | up

Fill in the correct phrasal verb for each sentence. Remember to adapt the tense of the verb when necessary.

(1) We ____________________ the neighbours' house while they're away.

(2) We must ____________________ before we make a decision.

(3) It wasn't such a bad experience when I ____________________ on it.

(4) ____________________ for the sign to the motorway.

(5) I'm going to ____________________ and see what I can find.

(6) I'll just ____________________ the trains to Shanghai in the timetable.

(7) Never ____________________ people less fortunate than you.

(8) He began to ____________________ a new job immediately after he was fired.

(9) I ____________________ meeting you next week.

(10) The manager promised to ____________________ the matter as soon as possible.

Exercise – Vocabulary Building – Phrasal Verbs with TAKE

B1 B2

Phrasal verbs are a combination of a verb and a preposition or an adverb. They are an essential part of the English language and are commonly used by native speakers. Phrasal verbs are extremely important for fluency when learning English and will greatly improve your understanding and vocabulary skills to communicate effectively. Note that each phrasal verb can have multiple different meanings.

Choose the matching preposition for each phrasal verb:

take __________	= become successful, flourish, leave	take __________	= understand, absorb, comprehend
take __________	= assume the job or duty of someone	take __________	= consider (mistakenly), regard as
take __________	= accept an offer, resume a task	take __________	= make notes (of information)
take __________	= accept responsibility for a job or task	take __________	= unleash one's anger
take __________	= dismantle, disassemble, criticize	take __________	= accept as payment

apart · down · for · in · off

on · over · it out on · it out in · up

Fill in the correct phrasal verb for each sentence. Remember to adapt the tense of the verb when necessary.

(1) Don't ________________ more than you can handle.

(2) There was so much information. I could hardly ________________ everything he said.

(3) They had to __________ the shelf __________ because it wouldn't fit through the door.

(4) The business had just begun to ________________ and will definitely make a profit.

(5) He will ________________ the job as managing director when Tom retires.

(6) Did you ________________ the key facts during the discussion?

(7) Don't __________ it __________ me just because you've had a bad day.

(8) I think we should __________ them __________ on their offer to help us.

(9) Don't __________ silence __________ anger.

(10) He agreed to ________________ merchandise instead of cash.

5 Conference Centres

Conference centres provide a business-focused environment. These facilities can be used for a variety of events: product introductions, press conferences, training seminars, motivational meetings, and new product launches. Conference centres usually provide accommodation, ensuring that your guests or staff are all at the same location. Meals and refreshments are part of their services, dispensing with the need for caterers.

Using such venues ensures you have all the technology you need to host any business occasion. Equipment available includes high-speed internet access, satellite video conferencing, and other means of presentation and communication technologies. These services are an extension of your office. The required equipment will be set up and a support team is on hand in the event of any technical problems. Additional equipment like notebooks, projectors and so on can be rented. Trained staff are present to ensure that everything runs smoothly. A conference service manager works with you and takes care of all the details, allowing you to focus on your event.

Most conference centres are within easy access of airports and train stations. Some centres provide transport for your attendees, for instance a shuttle to and from the airport. Furthermore, leisure and entertainment are not overlooked. Centres have bars and restaurants with meals of a very high standard. Sports facilities are also in-house, including gyms, swimming pools and saunas. Outdoor sports are catered for at some of the bigger centres and include team builders like rope climbing and orienteering, volleyball, basketball and of course golf.

Depending on your needs, centres will negotiate a price package, incorporating your requirements and the size of your group. This is beneficial as it means you can arrange the event to your specific needs.

There are a lot of advantages to using conference centres. You don't have to arrange accommodation, catering, transport and renting technical equipment. Staff from the conference centre will deal with any problems that occur. It saves you time, as you are dealing with just one company. It is more likely to be efficient, as your own employees are free to concentrate their expertise on your event.

Conference centres enable you to project a positive image of your company. Their staff are trained to set up these events and are experts in their field, giving you the opportunity to host a successful meeting, without the stress.

Answer the following questions.

A2

(1) Give examples of different events which can be held at a conference centre.

(2) What kinds of facilities and services are available in today's conference centres?

(3) What are the advantages of using a conference centre for your event?

6 Useful phrases for requesting information

With reference to your advertisement in last week's issue of the magazine Office Today, could you please send us a copy of your latest catalogue and price-list.

With regard(s) to your special offer/promotional offer on your website, we would be glad if you could let us have an offer for the goods/items/articles listed below: ...

Further to our telephone conversation of 15 July 20 ...

With regards to the visit of your sales representative, we would be grateful if you could forward us an offer for the following: ...

With reference to your current catalogue, we would be grateful if you could let us have additional information on ...

Further to our visit to your stand at the Cologne trade fair, we would be grateful if you could forward us an offer for the following: ...

Please forward us a copy of your current catalogue and additional information on ...

According to your website/leaflet/brochure ...

Exercise – Requesting information about a conference centre

A2

Sie haben die Aufgabe, Informationen über geeignete Tagesorte zu beschaffen.

Schreiben Sie eine E-Mail an das *London Business and Convention Centre* (info@lbcc.co.uk) und fordern Sie eine aktuelle Broschüre und Preisliste an.

Exercise – Deciding on a conference venue

A2

Background

Your company needs to find a suitable conference centre for its delegates.

	Benners	Meadowlands	Oakpark Inn	The Brandon	Horan's
meeting rooms	10	24	15	18	7
largest room (amphitheatre)	–	170	90	120	–
largest room (ballroom)	180	550	390	400	650
computer labs	–	2	–	1	–
guest rooms	70	150	120	170	140
guest suites	–	10	6	–	–
free Wi-Fi	–	✓	✓	✓	–
lounges	–	3	1	2	1
fitness room/ gym	–	✓	✓	✓	✓
sauna	–	✓	–	✓	✓
pool	–	✓	–	–	–
secretarial & office services	–	✓	✓	✓	✓
video conferencing	–	✓	✓	✓	✓
notebook rental	–	✓	✓	–	–
car rental	–	✓	✓	✓	✓
car parking	300	780	480	610	650
distance from airport	8 miles	4 miles	5 miles	2 miles	9 miles
shuttle service	✓	✓	–	✓	–
rating	** (2)	***** (5)	**** (4)	**** (4)	*** (3)

Assignment

Look at the table and answer the questions with a single word or figure.

1 Which centre has the largest amphitheatre?	
2 How many centres have a computer lab?	
3 How many centres have a pool?	
4 Which centre has more guest rooms than *Meadowlands?*	
5 How many centres don't provide free Wi-Fi?	
6 How many hotels have parking for more than 500 cars?	
7 Which center has the largest ballroom?	
8 How many centres provide secretarial and office services?	
9 How many centres have fewer than 15 meeting rooms?	
10 How far is *Meadowlands* away from an airport?	
11 Does *Oakpark Inn* have more meeting rooms than *Horan's?*	
12 Which centre doesn't offer video conferencing?	
13 Which centre is farthest from an airport?	
14 Does *Horan's* have a lounge?	
15 Which centre has the lowest rating?	
16 How many centres offer a shuttle service?	
17 How many centres rent notebooks?	
18 Which centre doesn't provide secretarial and office services?	
19 How many centres have more than 100 guest rooms?	
20 Could you rent a notebook at *The Brandon?*	
21 How many centres don't have an amphitheatre?	
22 Does *The Brandon* have a higher rating than *Oakpark Inn?*	
23 Which centre is closest to the airport?	
24 Which centre offers the least facilities?	
25 How many centres have no guest suites?	

Exercise – Booking a conference venue

A2

Background

You work for the company Walsh Technologies Ltd, whose head office is at 12 Broadwick Street, London W1A 2HG.

The Managing Director, Ms Jane Bristow, is planning to host a convention in Dublin. The event, which starts on 15 March, takes place over 3 days at the City Conference Centre. Jane has left the following note on your desk:

Hello, just a few points about the convention. We will need quite a large conference suite with a speaker podium including PA system and seating for 7 people on a stage. We will also require a notebook, a high-quality projector and an extra-large projection screen.

Contact Carol Baker at the Conference Centre. Ms Baker is in charge of bookings. Fill in the attached form and send it back to her by tomorrow. Ask her to reserve the Waterford Suite for us. We shall need the suite from 10 o'clock in the morning onwards and the finishing time is scheduled for approximately 1600 in the afternoon on the last day.

We expect around 250 attendees plus our guest speaker Dr Oliver Murphy. Please arrange for a car to collect him at the airport at midday, the day before the convention begins.

Remember to ask for the usual restaurant facilities throughout the event. Please arrange a coffee bar reception to start at 0830 and schedule lunch for one o'clock. I would be pleased if Carol could send me some sample menus to look at . Make sure they arrange tables in the restaurant to seat 6 people and ask for a wide selection of non-alcoholic drinks.

We will also need a large bouquet of flowers as a gift for Dr Murphy after his speech on the third day.

And don't forget accommodation for our delegates. Ask Carol to book five single rooms at the Grandeur Hotel. And, of course, an extra room for Dr Murphy.

Please remind Carol to send the invoice to me personally at Walsh Ltd.

Last but not least, I need a rental car, an estate model, automatic, to pick up at the airport when I arrive in Dublin. Please ask Carol to organize it.

Thanks!

Jane

Assignment

Complete the reservation booking form.

Dublin City Conference Centre

RESERVATION BOOKING FORM

COMPANY DETAILS: ____________________

____

____

____

CONTACT PERSON: ____________________

DATE OF EVENT: ____________________

NAME OF SUITE: ____________________

NUMBER OF ATTENDEES: __________

TIME: FROM: __________ TO: __________

MEALS: BREAKFAST LUNCH DINNER (PLEASE UNDERLINE)

TIME OF MEAL: ________ _____ _____

SPECIAL REQUESTS:

____

____

____

____

____

____

____

INVOICE TO: ____________________

Exercise – Organizing the collection of guests

A2

Background

Your company is hosting a conference in London, where you have to organize the collection of guests from the airports. Your manager has given you tomorrow's agenda.

"Seven people have to be picked up during the day. Ted Murphy is on flight EI 698 from Dublin, arriving at 0830 hrs at London City Airport. He called earlier to inform us that his colleague, Mary Lynch, is going to be delayed in Milan, and will not be arriving at Heathrow at 11 o'clock on BA 5869 as expected. He said she would phone later to confirm her new time of arrival.

Mrs Aysel Koç is travelling from Istanbul on flight TK1973 and is due to arrive at Gatwick at midday.

There are three guests to be collected from Heathrow. Arman Zayed, arriving from Dubai at 4 pm. The second guest is John Carter, flying in from Munich, on LH 412, due in at 1400 hrs. Also arriving in Heathrow is Mark Foster, travelling from Brussels on flight number QF 3404, arriving at half past six in the afternoon. Arman's flight number is EK 058.

Our last pick-up is at Stansted, at 1030 hrs. Pat O'Brien arriving on flight number TW 8346 from New York. He would like to be collected an hour later, as he has business at the airport.

Mary Lynch just phoned. She'll arrive at Luton at 8.20 pm on RA 704."

Assignment

Complete the list in order of pick-up time.

Airport Arrivals

Pick-up Time	Guest	Flight	From	To

Sample Checklist and Meeting Agenda

Event ______		
Main issues/agenda items: Date: Time: Location:	Notes:	
Person in charge:		
Attendees:	confirmed:	cancelled:
Mr/Mrs/Ms …	☐	☐
Mr/Mrs/Ms …	☐	☐
[…]	☐	☐
	done	to do
Book/reserve venue and facilities	☐	☐
Send invitations	☐	☐
Draft, compose and circulate agenda	☐	☐
Organize and confirm seating arrangements	☐	☐
Electronic equipment: notebook(s), projector, screen, printer etc.	☐	☐
Information materials, brochures, photocopies etc.	☐	☐
Stationery: notepads, pens/biros, markers etc.	☐	☐
Whiteboard, flipchart(s), OHP, screen, board markers etc.	☐	☐
Refreshments:	☐	☐
Additional requirements:	☐	☐

The agenda …

- ✔ includes date, time and location.
- ✔ communicates the topics to be discussed.
- ✔ provides an outline for the meeting.
- ✔ can be used as a provisional checklist to ensure that all information is covered.
- ✔ gives participants the opportunity to prepare for upcoming discussions or decisions.
- ✔ should be circulated approximately a week ahead of the event.

Agenda

Meeting of the IT Committee

Date: 25 August 20..
Time: 1400 – 1720 hrs
Location: Conference Room N02

(1) Opening
(2) Approval of agenda
(3) Approval of minutes
(4) Matters arising
(5) New user IDs and passwords
(6) IT infrastructure
(7) Software requirements
(8) Personnel recruitment decisions
(9) AOB (Any Other Business)

If you wish to add any further items to the agenda, please let me know before 21 August.

Eric Miller
IT Coordinator

Exercise – Vocabulary Building – Use these words instead of "very"

B1

"Very" is an extremely weak word, which doesn't communicate enough information. All it does is magnify another word. Therefore, you should use more sophisticated words to improve your English almost instantly.

Choose appropriate alternative from the list below:

very large	______________	very small	______________
very good	______________	very bad	______________
very cold	______________	very hot	______________
very easy	______________	very hard	______________
very hungry	______________	very thirsty	______________
very happy	______________	very unhappy	______________
very funny	______________	very frightening	______________
very rich	______________	very poor	______________
very expensive	______________	very angry	______________
very calm	______________	very excited	______________
very important	______________	very intelligent	______________
very old	______________	very careful	______________
very beautiful	______________	very ugly	______________
very clean	______________	very dirty	______________
very interesting	______________	very boring	______________
very friendly	______________	very mean	______________
very tasty	______________	very short	______________
very quick	______________	very sorry	______________

ancient	apologetic	awful	brief	brilliant	burning
captivating	cautious	costly	crucial	cruel	delicious
destitute	difficult	dull	effortless	excellent	filthy
freezing	furious	gorgeous	hideous	hilarious	huge
kind	miserable	overjoyed	parched	rapid	ravenous
serene	spotless	terrifying	thrilled	tiny	wealthy

B1

Translate the following sentences into English using some of the expressions from the previous exercise.

(1) Gestern war es **sehr kalt.**

____

(2) Die Prüfung war **sehr kurz** und **sehr einfach.**

____

(3) Das neue Design war **sehr hässlich.**

____

(4) Die **sehr alte** Fabrik war **sehr groß.**

____

(5) Ich war dort und die Geschäftsräume waren **sehr sauber.**

____

(6) Das Prospekt war **sehr gut** und **sehr interessant.**

____

(7) Das neue Modell war **sehr schlecht** und **sehr teuer.**

____

(8) Bitte befolgen Sie die Anweisungen. Sie müssen **sehr vorsichtig** sein.

____

(9) Es war eine **sehr clevere** Idee.

____

(10) Die gestrige Veranstaltung war **sehr langweilig.**

____

(11) Vergiss nicht, ihm die Notiz zu geben. Es ist **sehr wichtig.**

____

(12) Der Abteilungsleiter war **sehr verärgert.**

____

(13) Sie sehen fantastisch aus. Das ist ein **sehr hübsches** Kleid.

____

(14) Die Gäste waren **sehr hungrig.**

____

(15) Das Essen war **sehr lecker** und der Gastgeber **sehr glücklich.**

____

Exercise – Vocabulary Building – Forming Opposites with Prefixes

B1

One way to form the opposite is to add a prefix **(un-/dis-/in-/im-/ir-)** to an adjective or verb.

Prefix *un-*

able	–	**un**able
acceptable	–	**un**acceptable
achievable	–	**un**achievable
affordable	–	**un**affordable
afraid	–	**un**afraid
allowed	–	**un**allowed
altered	–	**un**altered
authorised	–	**un**authorised
available	–	**un**available
avoidable	–	**un**avoidable
believable	–	**un**believable
careful	–	**un**careful
certain	–	**un**certain
certified	–	**un**certified
changed	–	**un**changed
characteristic	–	**un**characteristic
checked	–	**un**checked
clear	–	**un**clear
comfortable	–	**un**comfortable
common	–	**un**common
controlled	–	**un**controlled
damaged	–	**un**damaged
defined	–	**un**defined
deniable	–	**un**deniable
documented	–	**un**documented
economical	–	**un**economical
edited	–	**un**edited
interrupted	–	**un**interrupted
known	–	**un**known
official	–	**un**official
specific	–	**un**specific
stable	–	**un**stable
usual	–	**un**usual

Prefix *dis-*

allow	–	**dis**allow
appear	–	**dis**appear
connect	–	**dis**connect
continue	–	**dis**continue

Prefix *in-*

accurate	–	**in**accurate
active	–	**in**active
adequate	–	**in**adequate
applicable	–	**in**applicable
appropriate	–	**in**appropriate
capable	–	**in**capable
consistent	–	**in**consistent
correct	–	**in**correct
decisive	–	**in**decisive
direct	–	**in**direct
effective	–	**in**effective
expensive	–	**in**expensive
sufficient	–	**in**sufficient

Prefix *im-*

material	–	**im**material
patient	–	**im**patient
perfect	–	**im**perfect
proper	–	**im**proper

Prefix *ir-*

regular	–	**ir**regular
replaceable	–	**ir**replaceable
responsible	–	**ir**responsible

Translate the following sentences into English using some of the adjectives from the previous page.

B1

(1) Das neue Modell ist **preiswert.**

___

(2) Das alte Fahrzeug war **unwirtschaftlich.**

___

(3) Sein Verhalten war **unvorsichtig** und **unverantwortlich.**

___

(4) Die Schätzung war **ungenau** und **unzureichend.**

___

(5) Die Änderung war **nicht genehmigt.**

___

(6) Kunden sind immer **ungeduldig.**

___

(7) Er war **nicht erreichbar.**

___

(8) Sie waren **außerstande,** das Problem zu lösen.

___

(9) Der Verlust war **unvermeidlich.**

___

(10) Die Zukunft des Unternehmens ist **ungewiss.**

___

(11) Das neue Modell war **unerschwinglich.**

___

(12) Der Vorschlag war **inakzeptabel.**

___

(13) Die verlorenen Daten waren **unersetzlich.**

___

(14) Die Vorgehensweise ist ziemlich **ungewöhnlich.**

___

(15) Die Produktion des Modells wurde **eingestellt.**

___

Exercise – Vocabulary Building – Phrasal Verbs with GET (1)

B1 B2

Phrasal verbs are a combination of a verb and a preposition or an adverb. They are an essential part of the English language and are commonly used by native speakers. Phrasal verbs are extremely important for fluency when learning English and will greatly improve your understanding and vocabulary skills to communicate effectively. Note that each phrasal verb can have multiple different meanings.

Choose the matching preposition for each phrasal verb:

get	__________	= have a good relationship with s.o.	get	__________	= escape punishment for
get	__________	= find out, succeed in discovering	get	__________	= retaliate, take revenge
get	__________	= move away, escape, take a break	get	__________	= successfully explain s.th.
get	__________	= be successful, make progress	get	__________	= return to
get	__________	= cope with, survive, be able to live at least at a minimal level	get	__________	= eventually begin or return to some procrastinated task

across | ahead | along with | around to | at
away | away with | back | back to | by

Fill in the correct phrasal verb for each sentence. Remember to adapt the tense of the verb when necessary.

(1) Anyway, I'd better ________________ work.

(2) Don't think you can ________________ with telling lies.

(3) I'll __________ you __________ for this!

(4) If you are willing to work hard, you will undoubtedly ________________.

(5) I need to sort out those files, but I haven't ____________________ it yet.

(6) We need to ________________ the root cause of this problem.

(7) How do you manage to ________________ on so little money?

(8) We've got lots of work and won't be able to ________________ before 8 p.m.

(9) My boss is a nice person and rather easy to ____________________.

(10) How can we __________ this __________ to the students?

Exercise – Vocabulary Building – Phrasal Verbs with GET (2)

B1 B2

Phrasal verbs are a combination of a verb and a preposition or an adverb. They are an essential part of the English language and are commonly used by native speakers. Phrasal verbs are extremely important for fluency when learning English and will greatly improve your understanding and vocabulary skills to communicate effectively. Note that each phrasal verb can have multiple different meanings.

Choose the matching preposition for each phrasal verb:

get	________	= complete a shift or a day's work	get	________	= understand s.th., catch on
get	________	= do or finish an unpleasant task	get	________	= continue, proceed with, begin
get	________	= be successful, progress with	get	________	= get organized, fix, rectify, get a grip
get	________	= escape or get a light punishment	get	________	= contact s.o. (often to ask for help)
get	________	= concentrate, start to direct your efforts and attention towards s.th.	get	________	= become involved in a discussion, issue, or activity

down to | into | it | it together | it over with

off | off | on | on to | on with

Fill in the correct phrasal verb for each sentence. Remember to adapt the tense of the verb when necessary.

(1) I usually ________________ at six o'clock.

(2) Oh, now I ________________!

(3) I ________________ him and explained our dilemma.

(4) __________ it ______________ quickly or you're going to lose your job!

(5) The sooner we start, the sooner we'll ________________.

(6) Let's ________________ business.

(7) You ________________ easy. You should have been fired.

(8) He's ________________ very well at school.

(9) Stop gossiping and ________________ your work.

(10) He was eager to ________________ politics.

7 Minutes of Meeting (MOM)

Minutes are the written record of a meeting and capture the objectives, decisions and outcomes.

The aim of minutes is to answer the following questions:

When was the meeting? (date, time and place)

Who attended? (a list of participants present)

Who was absent? (apologies for absent staff)

Did everyone approve of the previous meeting's minutes? (approval of the previous meeting's minutes)

Were there any open issues? Matters Arising (review of issues which originated from the minutes of the previous meeting; a list of things needed to be done before the next meeting)

Which topics were discussed? (issues, facts and figures)

Which decisions were made?

Which actions were agreed upon?

Who is to complete the actions and by when? (responsibilities and deadlines)

Was information material distributed?

Is there anything else? (AOB – Any Other Business: items discussed which were originally not on the agenda)

Is there a follow-up meeting scheduled? (date, time and place of the next meeting)

Who took the minutes? (name of the person responsible for taking the minutes)

Useful phrases for writing minutes

Mr/Mrs/Ms *[name]* submitted a report from/about ... containing details of ...

The subject/matter/topic/question of ... was raised/brought up (by ...)./It was reported/mentioned that ...

The advantages/benefits were pointed out.

The disadvantages/drawbacks were discussed/mentioned.

The following arguments in favour of .../The following arguments against ... were discussed/mentioned: ...

Mr/Mrs/Ms *[name]* pointed out/suggested/mentioned ...

After discussion it was agreed that ...

It was advised/recommended/suggested/decided/resolved that ...

It was decided/declined with a majority of 8 to 5 votes.

The vote/decision (for/against) was unanimous. It was unanimously decided to/that ...

The new procedure will be implemented by 30 November 20.../by the end of October/November/the year ...

Mr/Mrs/Ms *[name]* is in charge of/responsible for ...

The new campaign/layout/design will be presented by Mr/Mrs/Ms *[name]* on 25 August 20 ...

The concept has to be/will be adapted/adjusted/revised/modified/amended by ...

Remaining subjects were added to the next agenda.

There was no other business.

Sample MOM Layout

Minutes of Meeting of the IT Committee

Date: 25 August 20..
Time: 1400 – 1720 hrs
Location: conference room N02

Present: Baker, Bandler, Bristow, Gilligan, Miller, Murphy, O'Brian, Robbins, Stevens (see list of attendees)

Apologies: Allen, Norton, Smyth, White

Opening/Call to Order

The scheduled meeting was called to order at 1400 hrs on 25 August 20.. in room N02 by J. Bristow (Meeting Chair).

1 Approval of agenda

The agenda of today's meeting was unanimously approved as distributed. (see attachment)

2 Approval of minutes

The minutes of the previous meeting were unanimously approved as distributed.

3 Matters arising/Matters arising from the minutes/Open issues

All actions from minutes of previous meeting on 21 July 20 .. have been completed.

4 New user IDs and passwords

Mr O'Brian submitted a report on password security and its implications for the company. The benefits and drawbacks of new user IDs were discussed. It was decided that all staff receive new user IDs and passwords by 30 September 20... Ms Baker is in charge of implementing the decision.

[...]

9 AOB

- Mr Stevens suggested training for all staff to improve IT security awareness.
- Remaining subjects were added to the next agenda.
- (There was no other business.)

Closing/Adjournment

The meeting was closed/adjourned at 1720 hrs by J. Bristow (Meeting Chair).

Next meeting: 19 September 20.., 1400 hrs, room N07

Minutes submitted by: T. Robbins **Approved by:** J. Bristow

Exercise – Taking minutes during a meeting

B1

Background

You are attending today's meeting in room 107 and your task is to take notes for the minutes. The chairman William Gibson opens the meeting:

"Well, let's get started with our monthly marketing meeting. It's already three o'clock and we will have to finish at half four at the latest. What date is today? 21st? No, 22nd of March. Thank you.

I'm afraid Ellen Roslin can't be with us this afternoon, as she is away on business in Rome, visiting a new client. Also missing are Tom Peters and Samuel White, both ill, and Ted Miller, who is temporarily supporting the team at our branch in Brussels.

Let's vote if everyone agrees with today's agenda and the previous minutes ... Anyone against? Any abstentions? None? Very good; both unanimously.

Last month we decided to recruit an additional copywriter. Have the interviews been scheduled as planned? Finished? Well done!

Next on the agenda is our new advertising campaign. The Managing Director was extremely dissatisfied with the last agency. Therefore, we will need to hire a different advertising agency this time for our current campaign. Who is going to take care of this? Jack? Alright. Thank you. We'll need the quotes by the end of the month.

The next item this afternoon is our sales promotion event at the exhibition in Manchester. It went really well the last time. Ellen did a great job and she should organize it again, once she's back. When is the exhibition again? First week in July, isn't it? Right.

Then there's the issue with our new catalogue. Let's first discuss your ideas for the revised layout. Take five to list your suggestions on the flipcharts ...

I'm impressed! Excellent ideas. Our art director will be well pleased. Now we need someone to schedule and coordinate the photo shoot .... Rachel? Fine. Thanks a lot. Remember that we'll need the photos on the third of May.

I've received one item of Other Business. The photocopier in our head office is causing a lot of trouble lately, lots of paper jams and other malfunctions. I think it's time to purchase a new one. Let's vote. ... Unanimously, thought it might be. Kate, would you look into this matter and get details about three or four alternatives? You know, prices, features, warranty and so on. You could tell us about it at the next meeting. It's on the 24th of next month. But let's hold it in the conference room on the third floor, that's room 303, isn't it? It's bigger, less noisy and much more comfortable there. We should also start an hour earlier than today.

Anything else? No? In that case thank you for your contributions and let's call it a day."

Assignment

Use the information on the previous page to complete the minutes template below:

Minutes of Meeting of ________________				
Date: Location: Start time: End time: Chair:	Present:		Absent/Apologies:	
Agenda item	Discussion	Decision	Person in charge	Deadline
Approval of agenda				
Approval of minutes				
Matters arising				
AOB				
Minutes submitted by:				
Next Meeting Date: Start time: Location:				

Exercise – Vocabulary Building – Noun Formation with Suffixes

B1

One way to form a noun is to add a suffix *(-ility/-ity/-cy/-ness/-ance/-ence/-ion/icty/-hood)* to an adjective.

Suffix *-ility*

able	–	ab**ility**
accessible	–	accessib**ility**
accountable	–	accountab**ility**
available	–	availab**ility**
capable	–	capab**ility**
compatible	–	compatib**ility**
durable	–	durab**ility**
flexible	–	flexib**ility**
legible	–	legib**ility**
liable	–	liab**ility**
portable	–	portab**ility**
possible	–	possib**ility**
probable	–	probab**ility**
reliable	–	reliab**ility**
responsible	–	responsib**ility**
stable	–	stab**ility**
suitable	–	suitab**ility**
versatile	–	versat**ility**

Suffix *-ity*

complex	–	complex**ity**
intense	–	intens**ity**
productive	–	productiv**ity**
regular	–	regular**ity**

Suffix *-cy*

accurate	–	accura**cy**
consistent	–	consisten**cy**
efficient	–	efficien**cy**
transparent	–	transparen**cy**

Suffix *-ness*

appropriate	–	appropriate**ness**
bright	–	bright**ness**
close	–	close**ness**
correct	–	correct**ness**
dark	–	dark**ness**
effective	–	effective**ness**
useful	–	useful**ness**

Suffix *-ance*

abundant	–	abund**ance**
important	–	import**ance**
relevant	–	relev**ance**
significant	–	signific**ance**

Suffix *-ence*

competent	–	compet**ence**
convenient	–	conveni**ence**
dependent	–	depend**ence**

Suffix *-ion*

complete	–	complet**ion**
precise	–	precis**ion**

Suffix *-icity*

simple	–	simpl**icity**

Suffix -hood

likely	–	likeli**hood**

Translate the following sentences into English using some of the nouns from the previous page.

B1

(1) Der Bestellprozess ist durch eine hohe **Effizienz** gekennzeichnet.

(2) Unsere Kunden verlangen **Bequemlichkeit** und **Transparenz** im Bestellprozess.

(3) **Einfachheit** ist das wichtigste Ziel der Verbesserung.

(4) Die Reduzierung der **Komplexität** spielt eine wichtige Rolle.

(5) Die Lösung für das Problem ist von größter **Wichtigkeit.**

(6) **Genauigkeit** und **Präzision** sind die Voraussetzungen für gute Qualität.

(7) Das neue Produkt bietet eine verbesserte **Haltbarkeit** und **Zuverlässigkeit.**

(8) Wir müssen die **Abhängigkeit** vom Lieferanten reduzieren.

(9) Die **Verfügbarkeit** der Materialien muss sichergestellt sein.

(10) Die **Wahrscheinlichkeit** ist äußerst hoch.

(11) Wir sollten die **Möglichkeit** in Erwägung ziehen.

(12) Die **Fertigstellung** ist die **Verantwortlichkeit** der Abteilung.

(13) Das neue Werk hat eine hohe **Produktivität.**

(14) Unsere Produkte bieten **Flexibilität** und **Vielseitigkeit.**

(15) **Stabilität** und **Kompetenz** sind die wichtigsten Faktoren für den Erfolg eines Unternehmens.

Exercise – Vocabulary Building – Mixed Phrasal Verbs (1)

B1 B2

Phrasal verbs are a combination of a verb and a preposition or an adverb. They are an essential part of the English language and are commonly used by native speakers. Phrasal verbs are extremely important for fluency when learning English and will greatly improve your understanding and vocabulary skills to communicate effectively. Note that each phrasal verb can have multiple different meanings.

Choose the matching verb and preposition for each definition:

______________	= refresh, revise, improve	______________	= abolish, eliminate, remove
______________	= make sense, be plausible, ring true	______________	= quarrel, argue, have a row
______________	= compensate, make amends	______________	= encounter, run into
______________	= cause, facilitate, make possible	______________	= turn to, make use of, rely on
______________	= tricked, duped, be taken in, fooled	______________	= abstain from, forgo

add | bring | brush | come | do | do | fall | fall | fall | make

about | away with | back on | for | out with | up | up | up | up for | without

Fill in the correct phrasal verb for each sentence. Remember to adapt the tense of the verb when necessary.

(1) They are trying to ______________ much needed change.

(2) She's ______________ on her computer skills for the IT exam tomorrow.

(3) We ______________ against some unexpected problems.

(4) They might change the system or ______________ it altogether.

(5) The store doesn't have any. So, I'm afraid we'll just have to ______________.

(6) When he lost his job, he was forced to ______________ his savings.

(7) There was something about his story which didn't quite ______________.

(8) Don't ______________ her lies. She'll tell you anything to cover up her mistake.

(9) He resigned after he ______________ his boss.

(10) We ______________ lost sales by increasing prices.

Exercise – Vocabulary Building – Mixed Phrasal Verbs (2)

B1 B2

Phrasal verbs are a combination of a verb and a preposition or an adverb. They are an essential part of the English language and are commonly used by native speakers. Phrasal verbs are extremely important for fluency when learning English and will greatly improve your understanding and vocabulary skills to communicate effectively. Note that each phrasal verb can have multiple different meanings.

Choose the matching verb and preposition for each definition:

______________	= stop working, fail, malfunction	______________	= refuse, reject, decline
______________	= cause a delay, hinder	______________	= deal with, sort out, attend to
______________	= admit, confess, come clean	______________	= consult, ask for help, resort to
______________	= end, finish, close, conclude	______________	= adhere, follow, obey, abide by
______________	= succeed in reaching s.o., reach the same standard	______________	= doing something, occupied with (sometimes secretly, bad or illegal)

be | break | catch | hold | own | see | stick | turn | turn | wind

down | down | up | up | up | up | up to | to | to | to

Fill in the correct phrasal verb for each sentence. Remember to adapt the tense of the verb when necessary.

(1) Don't worry about … I'll ______________ it.

(2) That's irrelevant. Let's just ______________ the facts.

(3) I haven't seen you in ages. What have you ______________?

(4) Our car ______________ on the outskirts of the city.

(5) The company will ______________ with its competitors within a couple of years.

(6) Sorry I'm late, but I got ______________ at work.

(7) He was too afraid to ______________ to his mistake.

(8) They ______________ the offer then and there.

(9) She had no one to ______________ for support.

(10) I think it's time to ______________ this meeting

8 Writing Reports

A report is a systematic, well-structured document which defines and analyses a matter or problem. It is always written for a clear purpose and addressed to a certain audience. Specific information and evidence are presented, analysed and applied to a particular issue. The information has to be presented in a clearly structured format making use of sections and headings so that the required information is easy to locate.

Elements of a report

A report consists of the following 5 sections:

Terms of reference:	Why are you writing the report? Outline **what** the report is about and **who** it is for.
Proceedings:	Explain how the information was obtained, e.g. interviews, questionnaires, statistics etc.
Findings:	What did you find out? Present the facts provided by the information.
Conclusions:	Explain what the findings mean with regards to the issue or circumstances.
Recommendations:	Suggest suitable measures or solutions to deal with the matter.

Layout of a report

COMPUTER TRAINING SEMINARS

Milestone Systems Ltd

Terms of reference

The Managing Director, Sean O'Brien, has asked me to write this report on the proposed computer training seminars for members of staff.

Proceedings

A sample of workers and superiors was questioned and asked for their opinions.

Findings

- Most workers thought PC training seminars were a good idea.
- The majority of superiors expected an increase in productivity and efficiency.
- Some members of staff would prefer vouchers for external training seminars.
- A few workers suggested time off instead.

Conclusions

In general most workers and superiors were in favour of the proposed training seminars.

Recommendations

The proposed PC training seminars should be introduced for a trial period of 4 weeks.

(signature)
(today's date)

Additional elements in a report

In the case of detailed and extensive reports, the following additional elements might be required:

- Title Page
- Table of Contents
- Abstract (brief summary)
- Appendix/Appendices
- Glossary
- Bibliography

Tips for writing reports

- ✔ Reports have to be clear, concise and straightforward.
- ✔ The language in a report should be factual and neutral.
- ✔ Avoid colloquial language.
- ✔ Provide an appropriate title/heading.
- ✔ Always check spelling and punctuation.
- ✔ The report has to be signed and dated.

Exercise 1 – Reports

B2

Sie arbeiten in einem Unternehmen, welches Laserdrucker für den Consumer Bereich herstellt. In den letzten Monaten sind die Umsätze merklich zurückgegangen. Ihr Vorgesetzter, Thomas Burke, hat Sie beauftragt einen Bericht bezüglich der rückläufigen Umsätze zu erstellen.

Benutzen Sie die folgenden Informationen, um den Bericht zu erstellen:

Kundenumfrage bezüglich Qualität

„Sehr gut“	2 %
„Gut“	4 %
„Ausreichend“	31 %
„Schlecht“	48 %
„Keine Angaben“	15 %

„Wir haben oft nicht genug Leute, um die Produktion zu überwachen.“
(Mitarbeiter in der Fertigung)

Kommentare von Kunden
„... oft Störungen ...“
„... schon zweimal in der Reparatur ...“
„... würde ich nie wieder kaufen!“

Entwicklung der Reklamationen

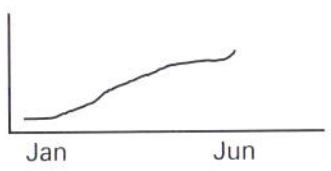

„Oft wissen wir gar nicht, warum die Fehler aufgetreten sind ...“
(Mitarbeiter in der Fertigung)

SYSTEMS Services Ltd

Exercise 2 – Reports

B2

Ihr Unternehmen erwägt eine Fusion mit einem Konkurrenzunternehmen. Der Vorstand hat Sie beauftragt, einen Bericht über die gegenwärtige Lage zu erstellen.

Benutzen Sie die folgenden Informationen, um den Bericht zu erstellen:

Umfrage unter den Managern

„Dafür"	28 %
„Dagegen"	38 %
„Enthaltung"	34 %

Kommentare von Mitarbeitern
„... das kann nicht funktionieren ..."
„... es wird nur Nachteile geben ..."
„... keine Vorteile für uns ..."

„Unternehmenskultur nicht kompatibel ..."
(Kommentar in den Printmedien)

„Nur minimale Synergieeffekte ..."
(Einschätzung eines Analysten)

Duggan & Sons Ltd

9 Describing trends and developments in graphs, charts and diagrams

When writing a report or presenting any kind of numerical data, e.g. the latest sales figures of different subsidiaries or personnel statistics of different periods, it is indispensable that you are capable of accurately describing trends and developments.

Study the following expressions and figure out their meaning:

Verbs to describe an upward movement
- to skyrocket
- to hockey stick
- to soar
- to shoot up
- to ascend
- to climb
- to rise
- to improve
- to grow
- to edge up
- to slope up(wards)
- to pick up
- to go up
- to reach a/its peak
- to recover

Verbs to describe a horizontal movement
- to stabilize
- to stay at the same level
- to remain stable/constant
- to level off
- to even out

Nouns to describe an upward movement
- an improvement
- an increase
- a growth
- a climb
- a rise
- a surge

Using adjectives/adverbs to describe the speed of change

steady – steadily
gradual – gradually
slow – slowly
sudden – suddenly
sharp – sharply
steep – steeply
rapid – rapidly
fast – quickly

Verbs to describe a downward movement
- to slump
- to fall
- to crash
- to collapse
- to nose-dive
- to plummet
- to plunge
- to drop
- to decline
- to deteriorate
- to edge down
- to go down
- to weaken
- to slope down(wards)
- to dip
- to reach a low (point)
- to hit a low (point)

Nouns to describe a downward movement
- a decline
- a decrease
- a fall
- a drop
- a dip

Using adjectives/adverbs to describe the extent of change

negligible – negligibly
slight – slightly
moderate – moderately
marked – markedly
noticeable – noticeably
substantial – substantially
considerable – considerably
significant – significantly
dramatic – dramatically

Useful time expression

In September .../In 20...
From January to March ...
In the first quarter/second quarter/third quarter/fourth quarter ...
Last month/year ...

Exercise 1 – Describing trends and developments

A2

Match the descriptions below to the corresponding charts.

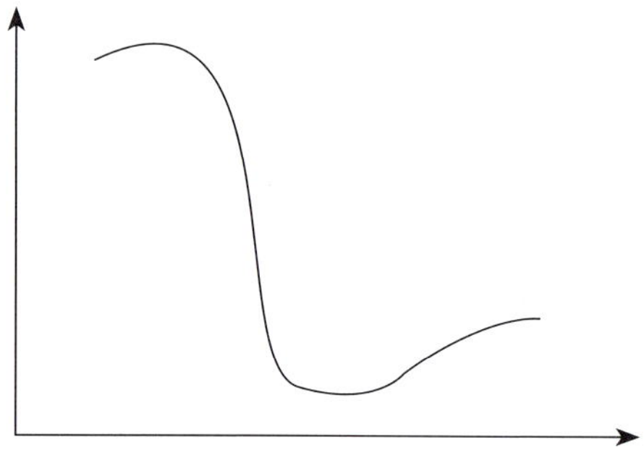

[ ]

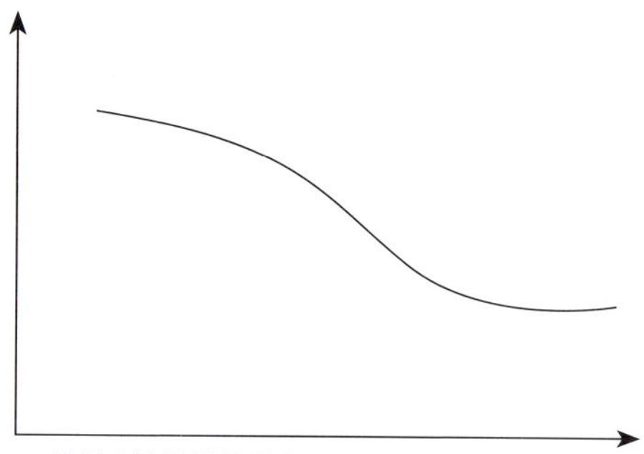

[ ]

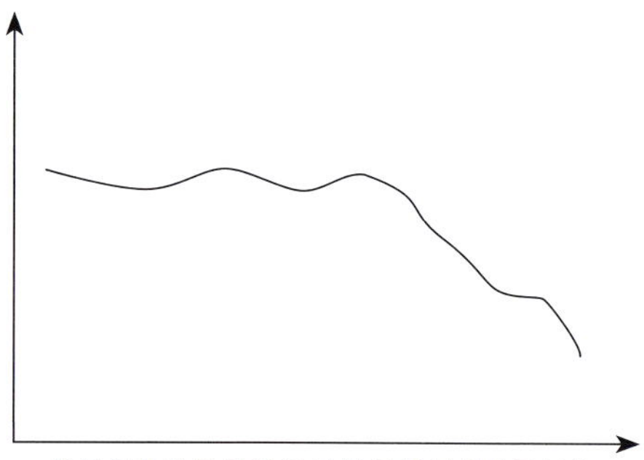

[ ]

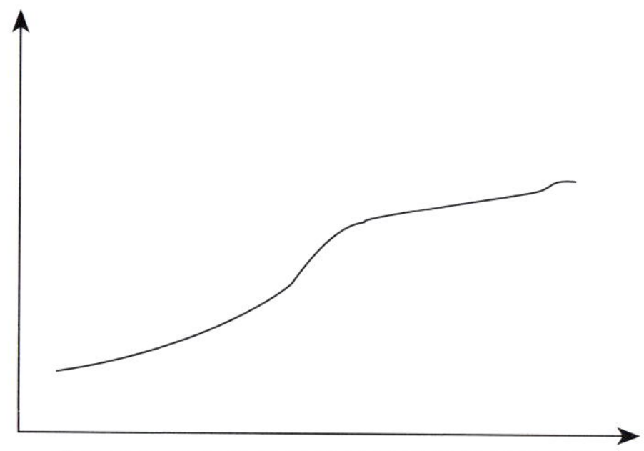

[ ]

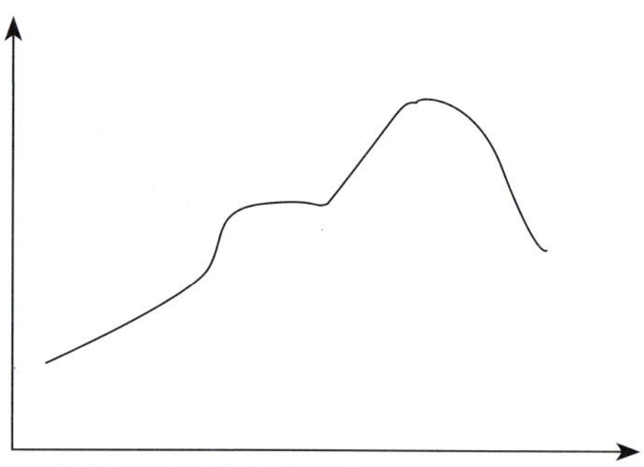

[ ]

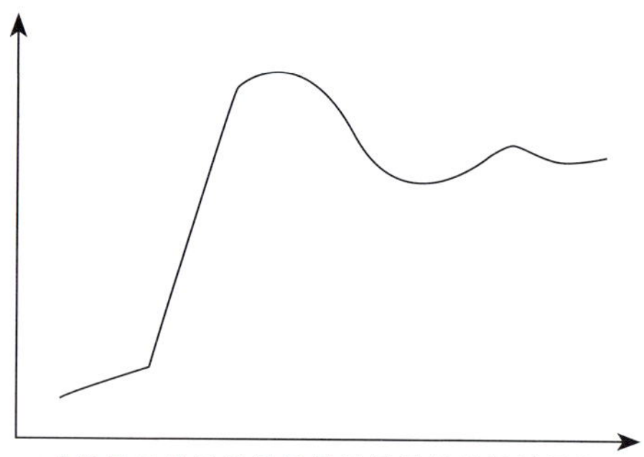

[ ]

There has been a steady increase in costs over several years.	Prices declined substantially before levelling off again in the fourth quarter.	Sales increased steadily, but slumped noticeably in the final quarter.
Share prices plummeted and hit an all-time low, before recovering slightly.	Prices skyrocketed, reached a peak before edging down slightly and remaining stable since.	Revenue remained stable in Q1 and Q2. However, in Q3 and Q4 it dropped markedly.

Exercise 2 – Describing trends and developments

B1

Describe the following graphs.

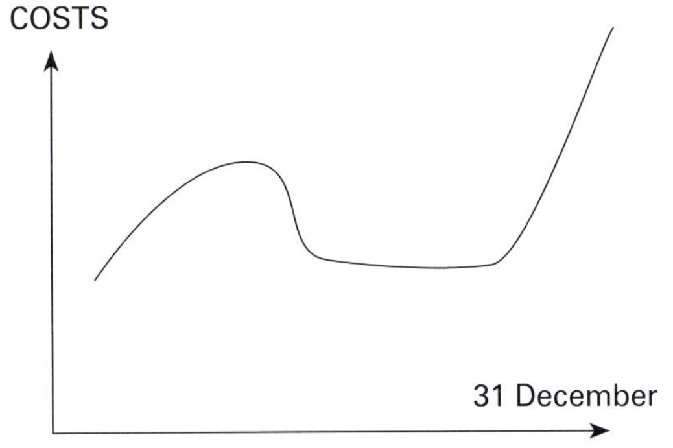

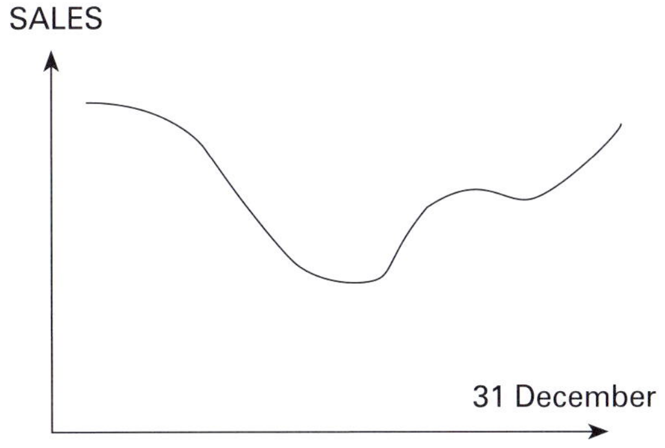

Exercise 3 – Describing trends and developments

B1

Give a detailed description for the development of the months from February up to December.

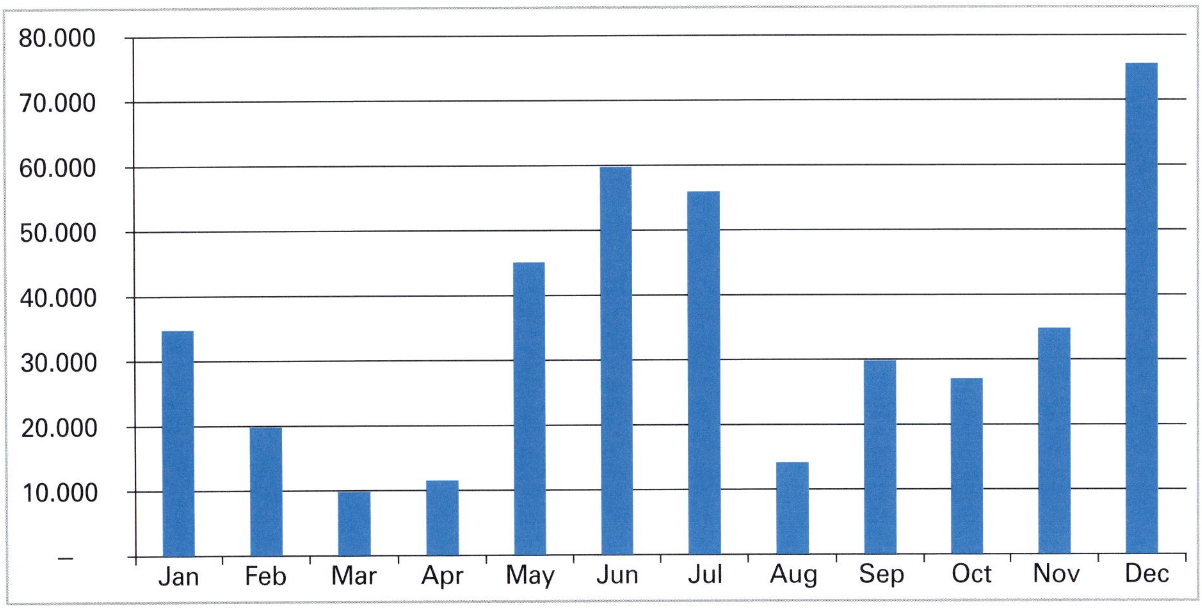

In January sales revenue was £ 35,000. In February …

Exercise 4 – Vocabulary Building – Binomial Pairs

B1

Binomial pairs are extremely common and powerful pairs of adjectives, containing two words which are joined by a conjunction (and, or). They must be learned as pairs, without any deviation or variation. The order is of utmost importance, like in "Ladies and gentlemen", "Fish and chips" etc.

Choose the correct "binomial pair" from the list below:

______________________	primarily, especially, above all
______________________	an assortment of small items
______________________	trying different methods to see what works
______________________	moving in one direction and then going the opposite way
______________________	occasionally, sometimes, from time to time
______________________	in many places, in one place and another
______________________	beside the point, unimportant, irrelevant
______________________	sometimes successful and sometimes not, not reliably good
______________________	invalid, having no legal force, no binding power
______________________	relationship of an action and its consequence
______________________	in a way that is slow, careful or gentle
______________________	plainly, essentially, fundamentally, without exaggeration
______________________	serenity, tranquillity, freedom from any disturbance
______________________	generally, as a rule, usually, on the whole, all in all, altogether
______________________	continuously, perpetually, without stopping, nonstop, uninterrupted
______________________	simple, common, routine, straightforward, fixed, agreed, decided
______________________	in a way that is easily understood, as clear as day, explicit
______________________	secure, uninjured, unharmed, unhurt, alive and well
______________________	healthy, well, fit, robust, in good shape
______________________	prime cause, ultimate, utmost, chief or all-important element

back and forth	be-all and end-all	bits and pieces	by and large	cause and effect
cut-and-dried	first and foremost	hale and hearty	here and there	hit-and-miss
loud and clear	neither here nor there	nice and easy	now and then	null and void
on and on	peace and quiet	pure and simple	safe and sound	trial and error

B1

Translate the following sentences into English using some of the expressions from the previous exercise.

(1) Die Besucher kamen **wohlbehalten** an.

___

(2) Sie entdeckten die Lösung **durch Ausprobieren**.

___

(3) Die Diskussion ging **hin und her**.

___

(4) Ob der Vorschlag tatsächlich angenommen wird, ist **unerheblich**.

___

(5) Die Botschaft war **klar und deutlich**.

___

(6) **Zuallererst** müssen wir eine Lösung für die Angelegenheit finden.

___

(7) Ein effektives Geschäftsmodell ist **das A und O**.

___

(8) Der vorherige Vertrag ist **ungültig**.

___

(9) Wir müssen den Kundenservice **stellenweise** noch verbessern.

___

(10) **Im Großen und Ganzen** lief alles gut.

___

(11) In der Schublade befanden sich lediglich ein paar **Kleinigkeiten**.

___

(12) Der ehemalige Geschäftsführer war **gesund und munter**.

___

(13) Nicht alle Kundenbeschwerden sind eine **simple und alltägliche** Angelegenheit.

___

(14) Es war **schlicht und einfach** ein Zufall.

___

(15) Es war eine Strategie **mit wechselndem Erfolg**, welche nur **hin und wieder** funktionierte.

___

Exercise – Vocabulary Building – Phrasal Verbs for BUSINESS

B1 B2

Phrasal verbs are a combination of a verb and a preposition or an adverb. They are an essential part of the English language and are commonly used by native speakers. Phrasal verbs are extremely important for fluency when learning English and will greatly improve your understanding and vocabulary skills to communicate effectively. Note that each phrasal verb can have multiple different meanings.

Choose the matching verb and preposition for each definition:

________________	= stop operating	________________	= reach end of available supply
________________	= follow, match, compete with	________________	= do and complete, a task
________________	= start a business, found	________________	= expand or extend one's interests
________________	= change for the better, reverse	________________	= become successful, flourish
________________	= enter, embark on, start	________________	= acquire, annex, take possession of

branch | break | carry | close | keep | run | set | take | take | turn

around | down | into | off | out | out | out of | over | up | up with

Fill in the correct phrasal verb for each sentence. Remember to adapt the tense of the verb when necessary.

(1) She is planning to ________________ her own software firm.

(2) The new service has ________________ in a big way.

(3) The building work was ________________ by a local contractor.

(4) She made an attempt to ________________ into accounting.

(5) Their business was ______________________ ideas, time and also money.

(6) A successful company must ______________________ the pace of technological change.

(7) Their plan is to ________________ the rival firm.

(8) The firm decided to ________________ its Paris branch for good.

(9) The new director successfully ___________ the company _________ in just six months.

(10) Many businesses are unwilling to ________________ into unfamiliar territory.

Exercise – Vocabulary Building – Phrasal Verbs for PLANNING

B1 B2

Phrasal verbs are a combination of a verb and a preposition or an adverb. They are an essential part of the English language and are commonly used by native speakers. Phrasal verbs are extremely important for fluency when learning English and will greatly improve your understanding and vocabulary skills to communicate effectively. Note that each phrasal verb can have multiple different meanings.

Choose the matching verb and preposition for each definition:

____________	= organize, prepare, arrange	____________	= succeed in doing s.th. difficult
____________	= exclude, reject, eliminate	____________	= plan and intent to achieve s.th.
____________	= develop in a successful way	____________	= postpone, delay
____________	= cancel an event or agreement	____________	= expect s.th. to happen, rely on
____________	= prove to be the case, transpire	____________	= prepare a plan, an agreement or other document in detail

aim · call · count · draw · line · pull · put · rule · turn · work

at · off · off · off · on · out · out · out · up · up

Fill in the correct phrasal verb for each sentence. Remember to adapt the tense of the verb when necessary.

(1) Bosses decided to ____________ the meeting which was scheduled for today.

(2) The solicitor has to ____________ the contract for the business deal.

(3) They were successful and ____________ the deal with the Chinese manufacturer.

(4) It's not likely to happen but we shouldn't ____________ the possibility.

(5) The meeting has been ____________ for a week.

(6) Things have ____________ quite well for us.

(7) We need to ____________ increasing sales.

(8) We can ____________ the support of our suppliers.

(9) The rumours of a petrol shortage ____________ to be a false alarm.

(10) I have a lot ____________ this week.

10 Choosing an appropriate communication channel

In today's business world there are several different communication channels available. Personal face-to-face communication offers many advantages. However, in a global marketplace, providing and sharing information often requires long-distance communication.

For written communication, it is still common to use ordinary postal services, i.e. sending letters. Courier services offer improved reliability, confidentiality, security and tracking, but these options are more expensive than standard everyday postal services.

Nowadays, speed is a crucial factor in choosing a channel of communication. Some years ago, sending a traditional letter was seen as reliable, professional and legitimate, but these days almost everyone has an email account and sending an email is easier and faster. Emails can be sent and received anytime and there is no need to pay for postage.

You can also attach presentations, spreadsheets and large documents, provided that the material is available in a digital format. Non-digital, paper-based documents can be easily transformed, as most modern photocopying machines can be used to scan documents.

In some cases fax machines are still used to transmit information. The scan-and-send technology through email systems has reduced the usefulness of fax machines, but they still offer a rapid document transfer and provide a true copy of a paper document. Furthermore, you obtain a paper-based receipt which can be used as "proof of sending". Moreover, sending a fax is faster and less expensive than using a courier service.

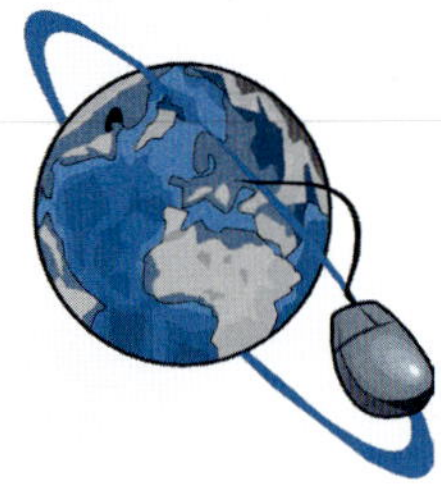

However, there are several disadvantages. A fax machine requires a telephone line and the device needs to be switched on continuously to receive faxes. Another drawback is that the archival storage of the printed paper faxes is quite cumbersome.

Modern technology has changed the way we communicate. Today's mobile phones provide internet access and offer sophisticated messaging apps. Voicemail messages, photos and videos are easily sent. Almost every smartphones also has a front-facing camera which can be used for high-quality video calling applications. Sending plain text messages already seems outdated.

A2

Give an appropriate synonym from the text for each of the following words:

today	__________	nearly	__________
fast	__________	better	__________
to offer	__________	choices	__________
furthermore	__________	old-fashioned	__________
machine	__________	regular	__________
disadvantage	__________	basic	__________
privacy	__________	duplicate	__________
nonstop	__________	daily	__________
numerous	__________	exact	__________
excellent	__________	advanced	__________
promptness	__________	nevertheless	__________

Essential Grammar – Comparison of adjectives

Adjectives with one syllable are compared with -er/-est.

(Einsilbige Adjektive werden mit **-er** und **-est** gesteigert.)

small	*smaller*	*the smallest*
large	*larger*	*the largest*
big	*bi**gg**er*	*the bi**gg**est*

Adjectives with two syllables ending with *y* / *le* / *ow* / *er* are also compared with -er, -est.

(Zweisilbige Adjektive, welche auf y, er, ow, le enden, werden ebenfalls mit -er und -est gesteigert.)

easy	*eas**ie**r*	*the eas**ie**st*
simple	*simpler*	*the simplest*
narrow	*narrower*	*the narrowest*
clever	*cleverer*	*the cleverest*

All the other adjectives are compared with more… / most ….

(Alle anderen Adjektive werden mit **more** … und **most** … gesteigert.)

famous	*more famous*	*the most famous*
difficult	*more difficult*	*the most difficult*
interesting	*more interesting*	*the most interesting*

Exceptions:

good	better	the best
bad	worse	the worst
much	more	the most
many	more	the most
little	less	the least

Translate the following sentences into English.

A2

(1) Standardbriefe sind **langsamer** als E-Mail-Mitteilungen.

____

(2) Kurierservice ist **zuverlässiger,** aber auch **teurer** als Standardpostdienstleistungen.

____

____

(3) Ein Fax zu schicken ist **schneller** als ein Brief.

____

(4) Kurierservice ist die **teuerste** Alternative.

____

(5) Einen Anruf zu tätigen ist die **einfachste** Option.

____

(6) E-Mail ist der **günstigste** Kommunikationskanal.

____

(7) Kurierservice ist die **beste** Möglichkeit in Bezug auf Vertraulichkeit.

____

(8) Standardbriefe sind die **schlechteste** Wahl in Bezug auf Geschwindigkeit.

____

(9) Kurierservice bietet die **höchste** Zuverlässigkeit.

____

(10) Videotelefonie-Anwendungen für das Handy sind die **modernste** Art der Kommunikation.

____

____

Exercise – Comparing parcel delivery services

A2

Background

Your company needs to decide on a suitable parcel delivery service.

	Premium Parcels	Nationwide Logistics	First Class Parcels	Fast Track Parcels	Express Parcels
Parcel Size S	$4.60	$4.80	$4.40	$3.90	$4.10
Parcel Size M	$6.90	$6.50	$6.40	$5.90	$5.20
Parcel Size L	$8.90	$8.50	$8.75	$7.20	$8.00
Parcel Size XL	$10.80	$10.20	$9.95	$8.90	$9.50
Oversized Parcels	✓	–	✓	–	✓
Tracking	✓	✓	✓	–	✓
Overnight Delivery	+ $9.50	+ $8.90	–	–	+ $9.80
Saturday Delivery	✓	–	–	–	✓
Pick-up Service	+ $5.90	–	+ $6.80	–	–

Assignment

Look at the table and answer the questions.

1. Which company offers the cheapest overnight delivery service?
2. Which company has the lowest rate for size M parcels?
3. How many companies accept oversized parcels?
4. Which company has the highest price for size S parcels?
5. Which company offers the most additional services and options?
6. How many companies deliver parcels on Saturdays?
7. Which company doesn't offer tracking?
8. How many companies offer overnight delivery and a pick-up service?
9. Which company has the best price for a size L item with pick-up service?
10. How much is the lowest rate for an XL parcel with overnight delivery?

1 Commercial correspondence

Layout of business letters

Sender's address:	Place sender's address at top right hand corner.
Date:	Place date at top right hand corner below sender's address.
Recipient's address:	Place recipient's address beneath date on left hand side.
Salutation:	If you know the person's name, use "Dear (name)". If you don't know the person's name, write "Dear Sir/Madam". If you are writing to a company or organization, use "Dear Sirs".
Subject line:	Placed between the salutation and the body of the letter.
Body of the letter:	Message, use full/complete sentences
Complimentary close:	After "Dear (name)", finish with "Yours sincerely". After "Dear Sir/Madam" and "Dear Sirs" use "Yours faithfully".
Signature:	Sign letter beneath complementary close on left hand side.
Typed signature:	Place printed name of sender beneath signature.
Position/Department:	State the position/department beneath printed name.

Caprica Office GmbH
Ritterstraße 12
40213 Düsseldorf
GERMANY
[Sender's address]

25 August 20..
[Date]

Classic Line Furniture plc
24 Meadow Lane
London N 17 9LN
UNITED KINGDOM
[Recipient's address]

Dear Sir/Madam [Salutation]

Information about office furniture [Subject line]

Please send us your current catalogue and price-list. We are especially interested in your range of open plan office solutions.

We look forward to hearing from you soon. [Body of the letter]

Yours faithfully [Complimentary close]

Steven Foster [Signature]

Steven Foster [Typed signature]

Purchasing Manager [Position/Department]

Tips for writing business letters

- ✓ State the purpose or subject right away.
- ✓ When replying to a letter, identify that letter by its subject and date in the first paragraph.
- ✓ Use paragraphs to structure your letter.
- ✓ List or itemize contents whenever possible.
- ✓ Place important information strategically.
- ✓ Include all the relevant information.
- ✓ Leave out irrelevant information.
- ✓ Find positive ways to express bad news.
- ✓ Focus on the recipient's needs and interests.
- ✓ Give your letter an "action ending" whenever appropriate.
- ✓ Check spelling, grammar and punctuation.

Caprica Office GmbH

Caprica Office GmbH
Ritterstraße 12

Sender's ad…

Classic Line Furniture plc
24 Meadow Lane
London N 17 9LN
UNITED KINGDOM

Recipient's add…

Dear Sir/Madam — Salutation

Information about office furniture — Subj…

Please send us your current catalogue and …
interested in your range of open plan office …

We look forward to hearing from you soon.

Yours faithfully — Complimentar…

Steven Foster — Signature

Steven Foster — Typed signatu…

Purchasing Manager — Position/Depa…

CLF
Classic Line Furniture plc

Classic Line Furniture plc
24 Meadow Lane
London N 17 9LN
UNITED KINGDOM

Sender's address

Date — 30 August 20 ..

Caprica Office GmbH
Ritterstraße 12
40213 Düsseldorf
GERMANY

Recipient's address

Dear Mr Foster — Salutation

Catalogue and price-list — Subject line

Thank you for your enquiry of 25 April 20 ..

Please find enclosed our current catalogue and price-list. — Body of the letter

If you require any further information, please do not hesitate to contact us.

We look forward to hearing from you soon.

Yours sincerely — Complimentary close

Allison Miller — Signature

Allison Miller — Typed signature

Customer Services — Position/Department

2 Anfragen (Enquiries)

Key vocabulary

wholesaler	Großhändler	to forward	schicken, senden, weiterleiten
retailer	Einzelhändler	to quote	eine Preisangabe machen
manufacturer	Hersteller	quotation	Angebot, Preisangabe
with reference to …	mit Bezug auf	delivery	Lieferung
with regards to …	mit Bezug auf	to take place	stattfinden
further to …	mit Bezug auf	willing	bereit
according to …	mit Bezug auf	to grant	gewähren
advertisement	Werbeanzeige	trade discount	Händlerrabatt, Branchenrabatt
to confirm	bestätigen	requirements	Anforderungen
leaflet	Prospekt	to receive	erhalten, bekommen
trade fair	(Fach-)Messe	efforts	Bemühungen
sales representative	(Handels-)Vertreter	current	aktuell

Key Phrases for writing enquiries

Einleitung (Opening)

- We saw your products at the trade fair in Munich last week/month/summer/April.
- We have visited your website/leaflet/brochure and are very interested in your range of products.
- We saw your advertisement for colour photocopiers in the magazine ...
- We have received your name from the Chamber of Commerce and Industry as suppliers of ...
- Your company has been recommended to us by one of our business partners/associates.

Ihr Unternehmen vorstellen (Introducing your company)

- Our company is a well-established wholesaler/retailer in ...
- We are a leading manufacturer of ... specializing in ...
- Our company offers a wide range of high-quality products, such as ...
- We are a rapidly growing company providing/importing/offering ...

Informationen anfordern (Requesting information)

- With reference to your advertisement in today's/yesterday's Office Media Journal, could you please send us a copy of your latest catalogue?
- With reference to your advertisement in the magazine Business World of 15 March 20.., we would be glad if you could let us have an offer for the goods listed below.
- Further to our telephone conversation of 21 June 20..
- Further to our visit to your stand at the Cologne trade fair, we would be grateful if you could forward us an offer for the following: ...
- With regards to the visit of your sales representative, we would be grateful if you could forward us an offer for the following: ...
- With reference to your current catalogue, we would be grateful if you could let us have additional information on ...
- Please forward us a copy of your current catalogue and additional information on ...
- Please let us have information on your prices and discounts/terms of payment and delivery.

Angebote einholen (Requesting an offer)

- We would be grateful if you could forward us a quotation for the following items: ...
- We would be glad if you could arrange to let us have an offer for ... as soon as possible.
- With reference to your advertisement in the magazine Business World of 15 March 20.. we would be glad if you could let us have an offer for the goods listed below.
- With regards to the visit of your sales representative, we would be grateful if you could forward us a quotation for the following: ...

Zusätzliche Anfragen (Additional requests)

- All prices should include delivery to ...
- Please quote all prices CIF Bremen/FOB Hamburg.
- Delivery should take place not later than 14 July 20..
- We hope that you are willing to grant us a trade discount of 10 % on list price.
- As discussed on the telephone, we understand that you will grant us an additional discount of 7.5 %.
- Please confirm that the equipment meets the requirements of DIN/ISO ...

Schlussformulierungen (Closing sentences)

- We look forward to hearing from you soon.
- We look forward to receiving your catalogue.
- Thank you for your efforts, and we look forward to receiving your quotation.

Sample letter – Enquiry

DV-ADVANCE GMBH

DV-Advance GmbH
Nibelungenstraße 37
95444 Bayreuth
GERMANY

17 March 20..

DS Documents Solutions Ltd
24 Meadow Lane
London N17 9LN
UNITED KINGDOM

Dear Sir/Madam

Enquiry

With reference to your advertisement in last month's issue of Office Proficiency, we would be grateful if you could forward us a quotation for the following:

2 Copy Star BW-6500i Black & White Photocopiers
1 Copy Star FC-8000 MFD/N Colour Photocopier
4 Print Star iQ 7055 Multifunction All-in-One Printers

We look forward to hearing from you soon.

Yours faithfully

Patrick O'Connell

Patrick O'Connell

Procurement - IT Services

Countries and their currencies

Country	Currency	Currency Symbol	ISO 4217 Code
United States (USA)	United States **Dollar**	$	USD
United Kingdom (UK)	**Pound** Sterling	£	GBP
Russia	Russian **Ruble**	₽	RUB
China	Chinese **Yuan**	元/ 圆	CNY
Switzerland	Swiss **Franc**	Fr	CHF
Turkey	Turkish **Lira**	₺	TRY
United Arab Emirates (UAE)	United Arab Emirates **Dirham**	د.إ	AED

Exercise 1 – Enquiries

B1

Ihre Firma, FlexPort AG, Lange Allee 168, 20355 Hamburg, möchte die Büros der Mitarbeiter neu gestalten und benötigt neue Möbel, insbesondere Schreibtische, Stühle und Aktenschränke.

Vor 2 Monaten haben Sie auf einer Möbelmesse in Köln ein interessantes Sortiment eines neuen Herstellers, NiceDesign, 16 Waterhouse Square, London N12 SLN, gesehen, welches Ihnen sehr gut gefallen hat.

Schreiben Sie an den Hersteller und bitten Sie um die Zusendung eines aktuellen Kataloges sowie einer Preisliste. Erkundigen Sie sich darüber hinaus über die üblichen Liefer- und Zahlungsbedingungen.

FlexPort AG

Exercise 2 – Enquiries

B1

Sie arbeiten für die Firma Meier & Wolf KG, Corneliusstraße 79, 40215 Düsseldorf, und haben in der letzten Ausgabe der Zeitschrift Office Today eine Anzeige der Firma StarSoft Ltd, 46 Longstone Rd, Edinburgh, Midlothian EH12 SNP, gesehen, welche eine neue Software („StarProject") für das Projektmanagement anbietet.

Schreiben Sie an das Unternehmen und fragen Sie an, ob von der Software eine Demo-Version verfügbar ist. Bitten Sie ferner um einen Termin mit einem Vertreter des Unternehmens, um weitere Einzelheiten zu besprechen.

Erkundigen Sie sich nach Rabatt für Mehrfachlizenzen *(multi-user licenses)* und den Preisen für Schulung, Wartung und Service.

MEIER & WOLF KG

Exercise 3 – Enquiries

B1

Ihr Unternehmen, Argus Computer Großhandel GmbH, Sonnenweg 40-42, 52070 Aachen, hat von der Industrie- und Handelskammer die Adresse eines neuen Lieferanten für Computerhardware und -zubehör, ProPC Ltd, 117 Swanston St, Glasgow, Lanarkshire G40 4HW, erhalten.

Schreiben Sie an den Lieferanten und bitten Sie um die Zusendung eines Kataloges sowie einer Preisliste.

Lassen Sie sich darüber hinaus ein Angebot über 60 Laptops mit 17-Zoll-Bildschirmen schicken.

Betonen Sie, dass eine Lieferung bis Ende des nächsten Monats erfolgen müsste. Alle Preise sollen einschließlich Lieferung nach Aachen angegeben werden; ein entsprechender Handelsrabatt wird erwartet.

Erwähnen Sie, dass im Falle einer erfolgreichen Geschäftsabwicklung weitere Aufträge folgen werden.

ARGUS
Computer Großhandel GmbH

3 Angebote (Offers)

Key vocabulary

enquiry	Anfrage	acceptance	Annahme, Zustimmung
offer	Angebot	as agreed	wie vereinbart
to submit	unterbreiten (Angebot), einreichen	as soon as	sobald wie
to refer to	sich beziehen auf	at the latest	spätestens
terms	Bedingungen	consignment	Sendung, Lieferung
enclosed	beiliegend, in der Anlage	premises	Geschäftsräume
goods	Waren, Güter, Artikel	valid (for/until)	gültig (für/bis)
to remain	bleiben	period	Zeitraum
property	Eigentum	to dispatch	verschicken, versenden
seller	Verkäufer	the above date	oben genanntes Datum
paid in full	vollständig bezahlt	Please note	Bitte beachten Sie
to increase	erhöhen, steigern	to point out	betonen, hinweisen
net	netto (ohne Steuern)	to hesitate	zögern
EXW	ab Werk (ex works)	in due course	zu gegebener Zeit
receipt	Eingang der Ware, Erhalt	to look forward to	sich freuen auf
in addition to	zusätzlich zu	on condition	unter der Bedingung
to settle	begleichen (Rechnung)	customer	Kunde
subject to	vorbehaltlich	while stocks last	solange Vorrat reicht
availability	Verfügbarkeit, Lieferbarkeit	to apply to	Anwendung finden
under separate cover	mit getrennter Post, in getrenntem Umschlag	without engagement	freibleibend, unverbindlich
subject to prior sale	Zwischenverkauf vorbehalten	unless otherwise stated	sofern nicht anders angegeben
to be effected	erfolgen		
Errors and omissions excepted.		Irrtümer und Auslassungen vorbehalten.	
Terms and Conditions of Business		Geschäftsbedingungen	
shipping and handling (S/H)		Versandkosten	

Key Phrases for writing offers

Einleitung (Opening)

- Thank you for your enquiry of 23 August 20..
- Thank you for your letter of 12 January 20.. enquiring about ...
- I refer to your letter of 22 February 20.. concerning ...
- Further to your enquiry of 18 March 20.., we have pleasure in submitting an offer on the following terms: ...
- As discussed on the telephone, we quote you for the supply of ... as follows: ...
- I am writing to confirm our telephone conversation of 30 April 20.. regarding ...

Anlagen (Enclosures)

- Please find enclosed ...
- Enclosed you will find ...
- We have pleasure in enclosing ...

- We enclose ...
- Under separate cover, you will receive ...

Geschäftsbedingungen (Terms and Conditions of Business)

- Our usual Terms and Conditions of Business apply.
- The goods remain the property of the seller until such time as they have been paid for in full.
- Products subject to availability, while stocks last.
- Errors and omissions excluded.

Preis (Price)

- All prices are net and subject to payment within 30 days of receipt of the goods.
- We are prepared to offer you a discount of 7.5 % on the list price.
- Wholesalers are granted a trade discount of 10 %.
- On an order of this size, we are willing to increase our usual trade discount of 10 % by a further 5 %.
- In addition to this volume discount, we allow a further cash discount of 3 % on condition that invoices are settled within 14 days of receipt of the goods.

Transport und Lieferung (Transport and delivery)

- All prices are (quoted) EXW.
- All prices are (to be understood) FOB Bremen/CIF Hamburg.
- The goods will be dispatched from our stores as soon as we have received your formal acceptance of this offer.
- Delivery will be effected once/as soon as ... we have received ... confirmation/payment ...
- As agreed, the consignment will be delivered within 14 days of receipt of order.
- The order will be delivered to your premises by 21 November 20 ... at the latest.
- The consignment will be shipped by air/road/rail/sea ...
- The goods will be packed in boxes, crates, cases ... measuring 40 x 60 x 80 cm.

Gültigkeit (Validity)

- This offer remains valid for a period of 4 weeks as from the above date.
- This offer is valid until 22 December 20 ...
- All offers are without engagement and subject to confirmation/acknowledgement.
- Offers are subject to prior sale unless otherwise stated.

Zusätzliche Informationen (Additional information)

- We would also like to inform you ...
- Please note that ...
- We would like to point out that ...
- In answer to your question we would like to inform you that ...

Schlussformulierungen (Closing sentences)

- Should you have any questions, please do not hesitate to contact us.
- If you require any further information, please do not hesitate to contact us.
- Thank you for your interest, and we hope to hear from you in due course.
- We look forward to receiving your order.
- We look forward to welcoming you as our client/customer.

Sample letter – offer

DS DOCUMENTS SOLUTIONS LTD

DS Documents Solutions Ltd
24 Meadow Lane
London N 17 9LN
UNITED KINGDOM

23 March 20 . .

VAT stands for **V**alue **A**dded **T**ax = Mehrwertsteuer
excluding VAT / exclusive of VAT / VAT exclusive = ohne MwSt
net = netto (= ohne MwSt)
in total = insgesamt

DV-Advance GmbH
Mr Patrick O'Connell
Nibelungenstraße 37
95444 Bayreuth
GERMANY

Dear Mr O'Connell

Quotation

Thank you for your letter of 17 March April 20 . . enquiring about our range of products. We have pleasure in submitting an offer on the following terms:

2	Copy Star BW-6500i Black & White Photocopiers	£ 3,299.00 each
1	Copy Star FC-8000 MFD/N Colour Photocopier	£ 4,699.00 each
4	Print Star iQ 7055 Multifunction All-in-One Printers	£ 555.00 each

All prices are excluding VAT and subject to payment within 30 days of receipt of the goods.

We are prepared to offer a discount of 2.5 % on condition that invoices are settled within 14 days.

The above prices are quoted EXW. Shipping to Bayreuth, Germany is £ 428.90 net in total.

Please note that shipping costs are not subject to discount.

This offer remains valid for a period of 4 weeks as of the above date.

Our usual Terms and Conditions of Business apply.

If you require any further information, please do not hesitate to contact us.

We look forward to welcoming you as our customer.

Yours sincerely

John Sullivan

John Sullivan

Sales Manager

Exercise 1 – Offers

B1

Sheila O'Donoghue von der Firma Walsh Bros Ltd, 12 Broadwick Street, London W1A 2HG, hat bei Ihnen (Weinberg & Partner, Birkenweg 4, 54294 Trier) einen Katalog angefordert.

Bedanken Sie sich für das Interesse an Ihren Produkten. Teilen Sie mit, dass ein Katalog und eine Preisliste dem Schreiben beiliegen.

Betonen Sie, dass Sie gerne weitere Informationen schicken, falls dies gewünscht oder erforderlich ist.

Weinberg & Partner

Exercise 2 – Offers

B1

Die Firma Net Log plc, Regents Place, 311 Euston Road, London NW1 3BT (Eileen O'Sullivan), hat bei Ihnen (CMC Hardware-Center, Kastanienweg 38, 63067 Offenbach) gestern telefonisch ein Angebot über 60 Laptops angefordert.

Unterbreiten Sie dem Unternehmen ein Angebot über 60 Laptops vom TYP DSX 6000 zum Preis von € 499,00 pro Stück. Alle Preise verstehen sich ab Werk.

Beziehen Sie sich dabei auf das Telefonat und bestätigen Sie die folgenden Details:

Zahlung per Überweisung innerhalb von 30 Tagen, 3 % Skonto bei Zahlung innerhalb von 10 Tagen, 12,5 % Handelsrabatt, weitere 5 % Mengenrabatt bei Abnahme von mindestens 75 Laptops, Eigentumsvorbehalt bis zur vollständigen Bezahlung, Lieferung innerhalb von 14 Tagen nach Annahme des Angebots, Lieferkosten € 99,00, Geltung der üblichen Geschäftsbedingungen, Angebot gültig für 6 Wochen.

CMC
Hardware-Center

Exercise 3 – Offers

B1

Sie arbeiten in der Vertriebsabteilung der Firma InfoMedia KG, Nobelstraße 16,93059 Regensburg. Die Firma OfficeLink, 12 Denny Street, Tralee, Co Kerry, Irland (Patrick Nolan), hat bei Ihnen ein Angebot über 100 InfoShare XL Organizer angefordert. Die Produktion des InfoShare XL wurde jedoch vor einigen Wochen eingestellt, da ein Nachfolgemodell geplant ist.

Teilen Sie dem Unternehmen mit, dass dieses Produkt nicht mehr hergestellt wird. Es wird jedoch in 2 Monaten das Nachfolgemodell geben, welches zu einem sehr attraktiven Einführungspreis angeboten werden wird.

Fügen Sie hinzu, dass Sie dem Unternehmen weitere Informationen zukommen lassen werden, sobald das Produkt erhältlich ist.

INFOMEDIA KG

4 Bestellungen (Orders)

Key vocabulary

to refer to	sich beziehen auf	as stated	wie angegeben
items	Artikel, Posten, Teile	shipment	Versand, Verladung
to supply	liefern	kind	freundlich, nett
samples	Proben, Muster	cash discount	Skonto
promptly	schnell, umgehend	to acknowledge	bestätigen
trial order	Probeauftrag	acknowledgement	Bestätigung
satisfied	zufrieden	requested	erwünscht, gefordert
to allow	gewähren, gestatten	due date	Stichtag, Termin
bulk orders	Großaufträge	shortly	in Kürze, bald
high-volume	große Menge	to place an order	eine Bestellung aufgeben
of utmost importance	von größter Wichtigkeit (von größter Bedeutung)		

Key Phrases

Einleitung (Opening)

- Thank you for your offer of 17 March 20..
- With reference to your offer dated 27 June 20.., we have pleasure in ...
- I refer to our telephone conversation of 23 February 20.., and would like to confirm the following details/order: ...
- We would like to confirm our telephone order for the following items: ...

Bestellungen aufgeben (Placing orders)

- We would be grateful if you could supply the following goods at catalogue price/at the agreed price.
- Please supply the following items, as listed in your catalogue: ...
- We enclose our order for ...
- Thank you for letting us have the samples so promptly. We would now like to place the following trial order.
- We were very satisfied with the trial order of ... and would now like to place the following order.
- We would like to add that delivery by the due date is of (the) utmost importance.
- We would like to add that prompt delivery is essential.
- As agreed, you are willing to allow us a discount of 17.5 %.
- We understand that you are willing to allow an additional discount of 10% on bulk orders (high-volume orders).
- As stated in your quotation/letter/fax/catalogue ...

Anfragen über Bestellungen (Requests about orders)

- Please let us know when the consignment is ready for delivery.
- Please let us know when the goods are ready for shipment.
- Perhaps you would be kind enough to confirm that you are willing to give an additional cash discount of 2.5 % for payment within 15 days of receipt of the goods.

Bestellungen bestätigen (Acknowledging orders)

- We acknowledge receipt of your order No. 2628 of 12 May 20..
- We would like to acknowledge your order for ... of 11 June 20.., and confirm that we can deliver by the date requested.

Schlussformulierungen (Closing sentences)

- Thank you for your efforts, and we look forward to receiving the goods by the due date.
- We look forward to receiving your acknowledgement of this order shortly.

Sample letter – order

DV-A

DV-ADVANCE GMBH

DV-Advance GmbH
Nibelungenstraße 37
95444 Bayreuth
GERMANY

29 March 20..

DS Documents Solutions Ltd
24 Meadow Lane
London N 17 9LN
UNITED KINGDOM

Dear Sir/Madam

Order

Thank you for your offer of 23 March 20.. Please supply the following items at the agreed price:

2 Copy Star BW-6500i Black & White Photocopiers
1 Copy Star FC-8000 MFD/N Colour Photocopier
4 Print Star iQ 7055 Multifunction All-in-One Printers

Please note that prompt delivery is essential.

We look forward to receiving your acknowledgement of this order shortly.

Yours faithfully

Patrick O'Connell

Patrick O'Connell

Procurement - IT Services

Exercise 1 – Orders

B1

Ihr Unternehmen (Vector Bürosysteme OHG, Opernweg 31, 63225 Langen) hat ein Angebot für mehrere digitale Farbfotokopierer und Multifunktionsdrucker erhalten.

Bedanken Sie sich für das Angebot. Bringen Sie zum Ausdruck, dass Sie mit dem Angebot sehr zufrieden sind und Sie es zu den vereinbarten Bedingungen annehmen.

Bitten Sie das Unternehmen (BlueLine Office Solutions, 27 Castle St, Eye, Suffalk IP23 7AW) um eine Auftragsbestätigung und um eine Benachrichtigung, sobald die Waren zum Versand bereit sind.

Vector
Bürosysteme OHG

Exercise 2 – Orders

B1

Sie haben von der Firma Milestone Systems Ltd, 6 Birmingham One Business Park, Clement St, Birmingham, West Midlands B11 2AA, ein Angebot für 25 PC-Komplettsysteme erhalten.

Teilen Sie dem Unternehmen mit, dass Sie das Angebot nur zu geänderten Bedingungen annehmen würden.

Fordern Sie eine bessere Ausstattung der Rechner (größere Monitore, bessere Prozessoren, mehr Speicher) und verlangen Sie einen Rabatt von 15 %. Teilen Sie dem Unternehmen darüber hinaus mit, dass Sie (Q-Tel Kommunikationssysteme GmbH, Am Neumarkt 23, 79115 Freiburg) eine Übernahme der Lieferkosten erwarten.

Q-Tel GmbH
Kommunikationssysteme

Exercise 3 – Orders

B1

Antworten Sie auf das Schreiben der Firma Q-Tel Kommunikationssysteme GmbH. Teilen Sie dem Unternehmen mit, dass die geänderten Bedingungen nicht akzeptabel sind und Sie den Auftrag daher nicht annehmen können.

Betonen Sie, dass Ihr ursprüngliches Angebot sehr konkurrenzfähig ist und ein ausgezeichnetes Preis-Leistungs-Verhältnis bietet. Sie wären allenfalls bereit, die Lieferkosten zu übernehmen.

Milestone Systems Ltd

5 Zahlung (Payment)

Key vocabulary

to suggest	vorschlagen	settlement	Ausgleich, Begleichung
terms of payment	Zahlungsbedingungen	to remit	überweisen
unable	nicht in der Lage	value	Wert, Betrag
favourable	vorteilhaft, günstig	invoice	Rechnung
at this stage	zu diesem Zeitpunkt	outstanding	unbezahlt, ausstehend
of good standing	mit gutem Ansehen/Ruf	to release	herausgeben, freigeben
bill of exchange (B/E)	Wechsel	cash in advance	Vorkasse, Vorauszahlung
draft	Wechsel	cash with order	Zahlung bei Auftragserteilung
sight draft	Sichtwechsel	cash on delivery	Zahlung bei Lieferung, gegen Nachnahme
letter of credit (L/C)	Akkreditiv		
crossed cheque	Verrechnungsscheck	remittance/transfer	Überweisung

documents against payment (D/P)	Dokumente gegen Zahlung
documents against acceptance (D/A)	Dokumente gegen Akzept
payment on receipt of goods	Zahlung bei Erhalt der Waren
payment on receipt of invoice	Zahlung bei Rechnungserhalt

Key Phrases

Einleitung (Opening)

- With reference to our order No. 17/280, we would like to suggest the following method of payment: …
- With reference to your order No. 258, we are prepared to offer you the following terms of payment: …

Zahlungsbedingungen (Terms of payment)

- With reference to your letter/fax/email dated 25 August 20.., we are willing to agree to the terms of payment you suggest.
- With reference to our telephone conversation on 26 October 20.., we are sorry to have to inform you that we are unable to offer more favourable terms of payment at this stage.
- We would like to inform you that deliveries to countries outside the European Union are only possible against an irrevocable letter of credit arranged through a bank of good standing.

Zahlungen tätigen (Making payments)

- We have enclosed our crossed cheque No. 355678895 for € 72,860 in settlement of your invoice.
- We have asked our bank to transfer the sum of € 24,710 to your account with the Deutsche Bank, Frankfurt.

Zahlungen erhalten (Receiving payments)

- Please remit the invoice amount to our account No. 344 771 with the Commerzbank, Alsfeld, Bank Code 51343224.
- We confirm receipt of your remittance of € 32,000.
- Thank you for your cheque in payment of our invoice No. 221/7840/03.

Zahlung mit Wechsel (Bill of exchange - B/E) und Akkreditiv (Letter of credit - L/C)

- This is to inform you that we have drawn on you a 2 months' sight draft to the value of € 28,000.
- We would be grateful if you could accept the enclosed draft and return it to us as soon as possible.
- Please find enclosed our invoice No. 221/7840/03 for €12,370. We agree to accept your draft at 30 d/s (days' sight) for the outstanding amount.

- We have asked the Deutsche Bank, Wiesbaden, to open and confirm an irrevocable letter of credit to the value of € 36,450 in your favour.
- We have instructed our bank to release the shipping documents against acceptance/payment of our draft.

Sample letter – acknowledgement

DS DOCUMENTS SOLUTIONS LTD

DS Documents Solutions Ltd
24 Meadow Lane
London N 17 9LN
UNITED KINGDOM

5 April 20 . .

DV-Advance GmbH
Mr Patrick O'Connell
Nibelungenstraße 37
95444 Bayreuth
GERMANY

Dear Mr O'Connell

Acknowledgement

We acknowledge receipt of your order No. 33 7/03 of 29 March 20 . .

Qty	Description	Unit Price	Total
2	Copy Star BW-6500i B/W Photocopier	£ 3,299.00	£ 6,598.00
1	Copy Star FC-8000 MFD/N Colour Photocopier	£ 4,699.00	£ 4,699.00
4	Print Star iQ 7055 Multifunction All-in-One Printer	£ 555.00	£ 2,220.00
			£ 13,517.00
		plus Shipping & Handling	£ 428.90

Terms of Payment:

Payment by bank transfer.

All prices are net and subject to payment within 30 days of receipt of the goods.
2.5 % cash discount on condition that invoices are settled within 14 days.

Please remit the amount to our account No. 887 447 338 021 with the Lloyds TSB Bank, London.

Yours sincerely

John Sullivan

John Sullivan

Sales Manager

Exercise 1 – Payment

B1

Die Firma PC Perfect, 31 Brearly St, Hockley, Birmingham, Westmidlands B19 3NS, hat bei Ihnen (Taunus Büromöbel GmbH, Feldgasse 17, 65222 Taunusstein) 40 Schreibtische vom Typ DS 8000 XL bestellt.

Erstellen Sie ein Bestätigungsschreiben unter Berücksichtigung der folgenden Details: Auftrag Nr. 388753/10, 40 Schreibtische vom Typ DS 8000 XL zum Preis von 329,00 € pro Stück, Lieferkosten 168,00 €, Zahlung mittels Überweisung auf das übliche Konto.

Taunus GmbH Büromöbel

Exercise 2 – Payment

B1

Sie haben von der Firma SalesCertified plc, Woodhall Business Park, Sudbury, Suffalk C010 1WH, Schulungsunterlagen für die Durchführung von Seminaren für Vertriebsmitarbeiter erhalten, welche Sie vor einer Woche angefordert hatten.

Bedanken Sie sich für die prompte Lieferung. Teilen Sie mit, dass dem Schreiben ein Verrechnungsscheck über 2.870,00 € beiliegt.

Bitten Sie um die Zusendung weiterer Broschüren für andere Mitarbeiterschulungen an Ihr Unternehmen (ProActiv Vertriebsgesellschaft mbH, Grundbergweg 48, 35428 Cleeberg).

ProACTIV
VERTRIEBSGESELLSCHAFT MBH

Exercise 3 – Payment

Das Unternehmen ProCert Solutions, 9 West Central Rd, Cardiff, South Glamorgan CF11 9HB, hat bei Ihnen um die Lieferung von 20 Laptops vom Typ SilverLine K7 CDL auf Rechnung gebeten.

Teilen Sie dem Unternehmen mit, dass eine Lieferung auf Rechnung in diesem frühen Stadium der Geschäftsbeziehung nicht üblich ist. Nach der erfolgreichen Abwicklung der nächsten Aufträge sind Sie (Hardware Center Dorsten, Industriestraße 22, 46284 Dorsten) jedoch gerne bereit, eine Lieferung auf Rechnung in Erwägung zu ziehen.

Bis dahin müssen die Aufträge leider gegen Vorkasse abgewickelt werden.

6 Versand und Transport (Dispatch and transport)

Key vocabulary

collection	Abholung	customs	Zoll
measuring	mit den Maßen	insurance	Versicherung
charges	Gebühren, Preise	taxes	Steuern
rates	Gebühren, Preise	handling charges	Umladekosten, Bearbeitungsgebühren
tariffs	Gebühren, Preise		
to advise about/of	informieren, mitteilen	door-to-door	frei Haus
to recommend	empfehlen	to look after	sich kümmern um
urgent	dringend	on behalf of	im Auftrag/Namen von
bulky	sperrig, voluminös	without notice	ohne Ankündigung
freight	Fracht	previous	vorherige
suitable	passend, geeignet	prior	vorherige
compared with/to	im Vergleich zu	plant	Betrieb, Fabrik
crates	Kisten	to take care of	sich kümmern um, erledigen
air waybill	Luftfrachtbrief		
bill of lading (B/L)	Konnossement, Seefrachtbrief, Ladeschein		
certificate of origin	Ursprungszeugnis		
insurance certificate	Versicherungsschein, Versicherungszertifikat		
rail consignment note	Bahnfrachtbrief		
shipping note	Schiffszettel		

Key Phrases

Abholung und Versand veranlassen (Initiating collection)

- We wish to send a consignment of hard disks to Dublin.
- Can you accept a consignment of 148 boxes measuring 30 x 60 x 30 cm for immediate collection?
- The consignment must arrive in Cork by 26 October 20.. at the latest.
- Please let us know your charges for collection and delivery.
- Please advise us of your current freight rates.
- We would be grateful if you could let us have your tariffs.
- We would like to know about your rates for urgent/bulky/large consignments.
- Please advise us of your extra charges for express goods.

Transport (Modes of transport)

- Which mode of transport would you recommend?
- Please advise us about differences between sea freight and transportation by train or a combined mode of transport.
- Do you think air freight would be suitable for the consignment?
- What is the fastest route from Glasgow to Cologne?
- How much more expensive is rail compared with road transportation?
- How long will the container take to reach Duisburg by sea?

Zusätzliche Informationen (Additional information)

- The goods are packed in crates measuring 60 x 80 x 60 cm.
- Please collect the goods from our Manchester plant by 0500 hrs on Friday.
- The consignment should be ready for collection by Monday, 25 August 20..

- We will take care of all formalities.
- We will clear the goods through customs on your behalf.
- We would like you to look after insurance and customs formalities.
- Please make sure that we have the documents by 28 October 20..
- Our rates include all handling charges.
- Our prices are door-to-door rates.
- Prices and terms of offer may change without previous/prior notice.
- Taxes and shipping charges vary and are not subject to discount.

Sample letter – Enquiry about collection and delivery

SYSTEMS Services Ltd

XPS Systems Services Ltd
12 South Clerk Street
Edinburgh
Midlothian EH8 9PS

phone 0131 355 1188
fax 0131 355 1199

15 January 20..

ProPlus Haulage Ltd
34 Castlebank Crescent
Glasgow
Lanarkshire G 11 6DU

Dear Sir/Madam

We need to send an urgent consignment of 40 photocopiers to Waterford, Ireland.

Could you accept a consignment for immediate collection?

Please let us know your tariffs for collection and delivery. Rates should include all handling charges and we would ask you to look after insurance and customs formalities.

We look forward to receiving your quotation by fax as soon as possible.

Yours faithfully

Donna Stone

Donna Stone

Dispatch Manager

Exercise 1 – Dispatch and transport

B1

Ihr Unternehmen (GreenLine Furniture plc, Fairgate House, 205 Kings Rd, Tyseley, Birmingham, West Midlands BII 2AA) muss 300 Stühle für die Ausstattung eines Tagungszentrums versenden. Beauftragen Sie die Spedition LongHaul Ltd, 58 Brearley St, Hockley, Birmingham, West Midlands B19 3NS, mit dem Versand der Güter.

Die Stühle müssen nächste Woche Freitag am Northwood Conference Centre, 164 Ashley Rd, Lee Valley Technopark, London N17 9LN, angeliefert werden.

Weitere Details bezüglich der Anlieferung sind beim Tagungszentrum zu erfragen. Die Rechnung soll an GreenLine Furniture plc geschickt werden.

GreenLine

Furniture plc

Exercise 2 – Dispatch and transport

B1

Ihre Firma (Desktop Software Vertrieb KG, Alter Markt 1, 74072 Heilbronn) beabsichtigt eine große Anzahl an Softwarepaketen zu importieren. Der Transport soll von einer Spedition (O'Connell Cargo Company, 64 Abbey St, Dublin) übernommen werden, welche die Waren in Dublin (RTC Software Engineering, 29 Grafton St, Dublin) abholen und nach Deutschland transportieren soll.

Erkundigen Sie sich nach der am besten geeigneten Transportmethode, den Preisen und Geschäftsbedingungen der Spedition.

Fragen Sie an, welche Dokumente für die Abwicklung erforderlich sind. Die Spedition soll alle notwendigen Formalitäten erledigen.

DSV DESKTOP SOFTWARE VERTRIEB KG

7 Verzögerungen (Delays)

Key vocabulary

concerning	betreffend, bezüglich	to make good	wiedergutmachen (Schaden)
agreed	vereinbart, abgesprochen	We trust that …	Wir hoffen, dass …
agreement	Einverständnis, Zustimmung	to look into	prüfen, untersuchen, nachgehen
unfortunately	bedauerlicherweise, leider		
concerned	beunruhigt	matter	Angelegenheit
condition	Bedingung, Voraussetzung	attention	Aufmerksamkeit
to expect	erwarten	to improve	verbessern
to confirm	bestätigen	improvement	Verbesserung
revised	geändert, korrigiert, überarbeitet	contents	Inhalt
to promise	versprechen, zusagen	to apologize	sich entschuldigen
serious delays	gravierende Verzögerungen	due to	bedingt durch, aufgrund von
dissatisfied	unzufrieden	severe weather	schweres Unwetter
to cancel	stornieren	breakdown	Betriebsstörung, Ausfall
unsatisfactory	unbefriedigend	hortage	Engpass, Mangel
once again	noch einmal, nochmals	to refer to so./sth.	an jmdn./auf etw. verweisen
haulier	Spediteur, Frachtführer	inconvenience	Unannehmlichkeit

Key Phrases

Einleitung (Opening)

- We are contacting you concerning our order No. 17/280, which has still not arrived.
- Although delivery was agreed for 8 June 20.., we are still waiting for our order No.17/280.
- Unfortunately, we have to write to you yet again about delays in delivery.

Beschwerden (Complaints)

- As our own customers are waiting for deliveries, we are extremely concerned about the situation.
- We have to point out that delivery by the due date was an essential condition of the order, and you accepted this.
- Please let us know when we can expect delivery.
- It is essential that the goods arrive by 2 July 20.. at the latest. We would be grateful if you could confirm this revised delivery date by fax.
- Unless you are able to deliver by the revised date of 2 July 20.., we will have to cancel the order.
- If this extremely unsatisfactory situation does not improve, we will have to find alternative suppliers.
- The financial loss caused by the delay in delivery must be made good by the supplier/by your company.

Schlussformulierungen (Closing sentences)

- We would be grateful if you would look into this matter as soon as possible.
- We trust that you will give this matter your urgent attention.
- We are sure you understand our position, and look forward to an improvement in future.
- Please confirm receipt of this letter and your agreement to its contents.

Auf Beschwerden antworten (Replying to complaints)

- We apologize for the delay in delivery.
- We were concerned to hear that your order No. 17/280 has still not arrived.
- We are sorry to say that we will not be able to deliver your order until 14 August 20.. at the earliest.

- Unfortunately, we have to inform you that the item you ordered is no longer available.
- The delay has been caused by factors completely beyond our control.
- The delay has been caused by severe weather conditions/a strike/a technical breakdown.
- The delay was due to a material shortage at one of our plants.
- As this delay has been caused by transport problems, we can only refer you to the hauliers/shippers.
- We will complete your order as soon as possible.
- We are doing all we can to keep delays as short as possible.
- We apologize once again for any inconvenience caused.

Sample letter – complaint about delay in delivery

Duggan & Sons Ltd

Duggan & Sons Ltd
7 Penston Rd
Glasgow
Lanarkshire G33 4AG

phone 01 41 417 8210
fax 0141 417 8211

8 Mai 20..

XPS Systems Services Ltd
12 South Clerk Street
Edinburgh
Midlothian EH8 9PS

Dear Sirs

Delay in delivery of order No. 17044/03

We are writing about our order No. 17044/03 which has still not arrived.

It is essential that the goods arrive by 21 May 20.. We would be grateful if you could confirm this revised delivery date by fax.

Unless you are able to deliver by the above mentioned date, we will have to cancel our order.

We trust that you will give this matter your urgent attention.

Yours faithfully

Sarah Forrest

Sarah Forrest

Purchasing Department

Exercise 1 – Delays

B1

Sie arbeiten bei der ProTec Maschinenbau AG, Industriestraße 76, 42651 Solingen, und warten seit 3 Tagen auf eine Lieferung von Komponenten für die Fertigung, welche noch immer nicht angekommen ist.

Schreiben Sie an den Lieferanten (Feeney Engineering Equipment plc, 6 Fitzroy Place, Glasgow, Lanarkshire G3 7RH) und bitten Sie um eine umgehende Stellungnahme per Fax.

Bestehen Sie ferner auf einer Lieferung innerhalb der nächsten sieben Werktage.

ProTec
Maschinenbau AG

Exercise 2 – Delays

B1

Nach acht Werktagen hat sich das Unternehmen Feeney Engineering Equipment plc noch immer nicht gemeldet. Teilen Sie dem Unternehmen mit, dass Sie die Komponenten anderweitig beschaffen werden und Sie den Auftrag leider stornieren müssen.

ProTec
Maschinenbau AG

Exercise 3 – Delays

B1

Als Leiter der Kundenbetreuung der Firma Feeney Engineering Equipment plc haben Sie von dem Vorfall mit der ProTec Maschinenbau AG erfahren.

Antworten Sie auf die Beschwerde des Unternehmens. Entschuldigen Sie sich für die Verspätung und begründen Sie die Verzögerung mit technischen Problemen, die in der Zwischenzeit beseitigt wurden.

Betonen Sie, dass derartige Verspätungen in Zukunft nicht mehr auftreten werden.

Ferner haben Sie mit den verantwortlichen Mitarbeitern in den Bereichen Beschaffung, Logistik und Versand gesprochen, um Verbesserungen anzuregen.

Bringen Sie darüber hinaus Ihre Hoffnung zum Ausdruck, das Unternehmen trotz der Probleme weiterhin als Kunden begrüßen zu können.

FEENEY
Engineering Equipment plc

8 Mangelhafte Lieferung (Bad delivery)

Key vocabulary

to complain	sich beschweren, reklamieren
to draw attention	Aufmerksamkeit auf etwas lenken
to express	zum Ausdruck bringen
dissatisfaction	Unzufriedenheit
packing	Verpackung
damaged	beschädigt
faulty	fehlerhaft, mangelhaft
poor quality	schlechte Qualität
to comply with	entsprechen, erfüllen
specifications	Vorgaben, Anforderungen
incomplete	unvollständig
missing	fehlend
to return	zurückschicken
to expect	erwarten
refund	Rückerstattung
to replace	ersetzen, austauschen
replacements	Ersatz
at your expense	auf Ihre Kosten
to obtain	beschaffen, beziehen, erhalten, bekommen
to deduct	abziehen
already	bereits, schon
substandard	minderwertig, Ausschuss
records	Aufzeichnungen, Unterlagen
examined	geprüft, untersucht
to conform to	entsprechen, übereinstimmen mit
claim	Forderung, Beanstandung
to propose	beabsichtigen, vorschlagen

Key Phrases

Einleitung (Opening)

- I am writing to complain about ...
- We wish to inform you that ...
- I am writing to inform you that ...
- I wish to draw your attention to ...
- We are writing to express our dissatisfaction with ...

Problem beschreiben (Describing the problem)

- The packing was damaged.
- The supplied components are damaged/defective/faulty/of poor quality.
- The supplied items did not comply with our quality specifications.
- On checking the consignment, we found it to be incomplete. The following items are missing: ...
- You have obviously made a mistake and sent us the wrong items.

Forderungen stellen (Making claims)

- We have arranged for the goods to be returned to you and expect a full refund without delay.
- Please send us the missing items as soon as possible.
- We have arranged to obtain the missing items elsewhere and will deduct them from your invoice.
- We have arranged for the defective items to be returned to you at your expense and hope to receive replacements without delay.

Ansprüche akzeptieren (Accepting claims)

- We are sorry about our mistake/the problem, and we have already dispatched the correct articles.
- We regret that you have received the wrong articles/substandard goods/faulty components and we will of course replace them at our expense.
- We apologize for any inconvenience caused.

Ansprüche ablehnen (Rejecting claims)

- There seems to have been a misunderstanding. According to our records (order No. 17/280), the consignment is complete.
- Our department has examined the components and they conform to specification in every way.
- We are sure that you will understand our reasons for not accepting your claim.

Schlussformulierungen (Closing sentences)

- Please let me know as soon as possible what action you propose to take.
- I hope we can settle this matter to our satisfaction.

Sample letter – Complaint about defective goods

ITT Direct

ITT Direct
7 Clash Rd
Tralee
County Kerry
IRELAND (EIRE)

17 March 20..

JPG Tech Solutions Ltd
232 Bryant Park Lane
London N 17 9LN
UNITED KINGDOM

Dear Sir/Madam

Complaint about defective items

We are writing to express our dissatisfaction with your latest delivery.

On checking the consignment, we found that almost half of the supplied components were badly damaged.

We have arranged for the defective items to be returned to you at your expense and hope to receive replacements without delay.

We look forward to hearing from you soon.

Yours faithfully

Oliver Murphy

Oliver Murphy

Purchasing Department

Exercise 1 – Bad delivery

B1

Ihr Unternehmen (Westland Office GmbH & Co KG, Schlossallee 16, 89231 Neu-Ulm) hat von einem Händler 50 Laptops eingekauft.

Bei der Wareneingangskontrolle mussten Sie jedoch feststellen, dass 7 der Laptops beschädigt sind, was vermutlich auf eine unzureichende Verpackung zurückzuführen ist.

Schreiben Sie an den Lieferanten (ICB Hardware Ltd, 9 Wicklow St, Dublin, Ireland), reklamieren Sie die Lieferung und fordern Sie Ersatz für die beschädigten Geräte.

WESTLANDOFFICE

GmbH & Co. KG

Exercise 2 – Bad delivery

B1

Antworten Sie auf die Reklamation des Unternehmens Westland IT GmbH & Co KG. Entschuldigen Sie sich für die mangelhafte Lieferung und sichern Sie dem Unternehmen eine umgehende Ersatzlieferung zu.

ICB Hardware Ltd

Exercise 3 – Bad delivery

B1

Letzte Woche hat Ihre Firma (DuraPrint OHG, Am Südhang 18, 66121 Saarbrücken) von Ihrem Händler eine Lieferung Druckerzubehör erhalten. Beim Auspacken mussten Sie jedoch feststellen, dass die falschen Druckerpatronen (printer cartridges) geliefert wurden. Die darüber hinaus bestellten Druckerkabel fehlten komplett.

Schreiben Sie an den Händler (O'Grady Print Supplies Ltd, 4 Breydon Avenue, Cusworth Lane, Doncaster DN5 8LA) und beanstanden Sie die Falschlieferung.

DuraPrint OHG

Exercise 4 – Bad delivery

B1

Sie haben von der Firma CD Centre, 510 Oxford St, London W1C 2PZ eine Reklamation über eine Falschlieferung erhalten. Der zuständige Sachbearbeiter in Ihrem Unternehmen, Kevin Breen, hat Ihnen jedoch versichert, dass die Bestellung ordnungsgemäß abgewickelt wurde.

Antworten Sie (Remmert Audio Technik KG, Nordring 7, 38102 Braunschweig) auf die Reklamation und teilen Sie dem Unternehmen mit, dass alle bestellten Artikel (Bestellung Nr. 221/498/0703) ordnungsgemäß verpackt und verschickt wurden.

Alle Sendungen werden darüber hinaus vor dem Verlassen der Versandabteilung noch einmal überprüft.

Remmert
Audio Technik KG

9 Mahnungen (Reminders)

Key vocabulary

overlooked	übersehen	to insist on	auf etw. bestehen
statement of account	Kontoauszug, Abrechnung	to start proceedings	gerichtliche Schritte unternehmen
overdue	überfällig	solicitor	Anwalt, Rechtsanwalt
balance	Saldo, Differenz	with regret	mit Bedauern
despite	trotz	in the meantime	in der Zwischenzeit
to remind	jmdn. erinnern	immediate settlement	sofortige Begleichung
confidently	zuversichtlich		
to cover	decken, abdecken		
ample	reichlich, genügend		

Key Phrases

Einleitung (Opening)

- We are contacting you regarding our invoice of 25 May 20.., which you still have not settled.
- We are writing concerning our invoice of 25 May 20.., which we feel sure you have overlooked.
- You may have overlooked our statement of account.
- Please note that your invoice No. 883/03 is overdue.
- You may have overlooked that a balance of € 625.00 is still open on your account.
- It has come to our attention that you still have not settled our invoice of 25 May 20.., despite our reminder.
- We are writing for a third time concerning our invoice dated 25 May 20.., which is still outstanding.

Zahlung verlangen (Demanding payment)

- We are sure that you will settle the invoice now that we have reminded you about it.
- Now that we have reminded you a second time we confidently expect your remittance.
- After this second reminder, we expect payment by 30 June 20..
- We must ask you to remit the amount covering your current due account.
- You have not reacted to our previous reminders, although we gave you ample time to pay. Now we must insist on payment in full within 10 days.

Weitere Maßnahmen (Further action)

- Unless we receive payment in full by 21 July 20.. we will start proceedings without further notice.
- Unless we receive payment in full by 21 July 20.. we will have no choice but to place the matter with our solicitors.
- We regret to inform you that unless we receive payment in full by 21 July 20..; the matter will be placed with our solicitors.

Schlussformulierungen (Closing sentences)

- If you have settled the invoice in the meantime, please ignore this letter.
- We look forward to receiving payment within the next few days.
- We look forward to receiving your remittance soon.
- We are sure that no further reminder will be necessary and look forward to an immediate settlement.

Sample letter – Reminder

VPN Services Ltd
47 West Street
Edinburgh
Midlothian EHB 9PS

16 April 20..

CS Office Systems
Mrs Carol Scott
27 Windsor Rd
Manchester
Lancashire M19 2EB

Dear Mrs Scott

Non-payment of invoice No. 44719/EOB/03

We are writing concerning our invoice No. 44719/EOB/03 dated 12 February 20.., which is still outstanding.

Please remit the invoice amount of £ 348.00 to our account No. 499 732 110 with the Abbey National Bank, Edinburgh.

If you have settled the invoice in the meantime, please ignore this letter.

Yours sincerely

Eric Stewart

Eric Stewart

Customer Accounts

Exercise 1 – Reminders

B1

Sie arbeiten in der Buchhaltungsabteilung der Firma Huber & Co. KG, Südwall 27, 90489 Nürnberg. Ein langjähriger Kunde, Sean Murphy, 11 Bridle Lane, London W1R 3HL, hat seine Rechnung vom letzten Monat noch nicht bezahlt.

Schreiben Sie eine erste Zahlungserinnerung und bitten Sie um die Überweisung des ausstehenden Betrages von 310,00 €.

Huber & Co. KG

Exercise 2 – Reminders

B1

Sie sind Geschäftsführer der Firma Fischer Bürosysteme OHG, Am Wall 23, 23554 Lübeck.

Schreiben Sie eine zweite Mahnung an das Unternehmen FX Supplies Ltd, PO Box 37, Manchester, Lancashire M60 1BZ, bezüglich der noch ausstehenden Rechnung (Nr. 6231/3) über 12.340,00 €.

Fordern Sie das Unternehmen auf, die Rechnung innerhalb von 3 Wochen zu begleichen.

Fischer Bürosysteme OHG

Exercise 3 – Reminders

B1

Schreiben Sie als Geschäftsführer der Firma Fischer Bürosysteme OHG eine letzte Mahnung an das Unternehmen FX Supplies Ltd bezüglich der noch ausstehenden Rechnung (Nr. 6231/3) über 12.340,00 €.

Drohen Sie dem Unternehmen mit Konsequenzen und machen Sie deutlich, dass Sie umgehend rechtliche Schritte einleiten werden, falls die Zahlung nicht innerhalb der nächsten 10 Tage erfolgt.

Fischer Bürosysteme OHG

Exercise 4 – Reminders

B1

Sie arbeiten in der Buchhaltung der Firma ProShop GmbH, Ringstraße 81, 91052 Erlangen.

Sie haben von dem Unternehmen ComLine plc, 82 Barrack Rd, Guildford, Surrey GU2 9ZW, irrtümlicherweise eine Mahnung bezüglich der Rechnung Nr. 112/84603 erhalten.

Teilen Sie dem Unternehmen mit, dass die Rechnung bereits vor 3 Wochen beglichen wurde.

ProShop GmbH

Unit 4: Kunden akquirieren und binden

1 Writing Sales Letters

Sales letters are used to introduce products or services to a new potential customer. However, the main purpose of sales letters is not to sell the product. A good sales letter is a "door opener". It is a chance to generate a response, e.g. a reply card, an email, a fax or a phone call.

How to write effective sales letters

- ✔ Begin by describing a frequent problem which the prospect needs to solve. Then present your product which will provide the solution to the problem.
- ✔ It's important to quickly move to your "sales pitch" in your sales letter. Don't waste the reader's time. Get to the point and limit the sales letter to one page max.
- ✔ Focus on the needs of the recipient. What does the prospect need?
- ✔ Structure your letter, using an introduction, a body and a conclusion. In the introduction, say why you're sending the letter. The body is your "sales pitch", where you'll explain why your offer is irresistible. The conclusion summarizes the main benefits, asking the customer to take advantage of the offer.
- ✔ Make it easy to read and keep it personal and conversational. Use short sentences and short paragraphs. Avoid a huge "wall of text". People like to have breaks in their reading, so-called "white space". Be clear and concise and get to the point. Say who you are, what you do, how you can help with the issue and how to get in touch with you. If it doesn't sound smoothly and naturally, you should revise or rewrite it.
- ✔ Be the customer as you write. Imagine yourself as the reader of your own sales letter and include the information the customer wants to know – not what you want to say.
- ✔ Make your letter as long as it needs to be. When asked how long a man's legs should be, the American President Abraham Lincoln once replied, „Long enough to reach the ground." It is the same with your sales letter. It should be just as long as it needs to be. No more. No less.
- ✔ Always appear credible and professional in the presentation and content of your sales letter.
- ✔ Sell benefits, not features! Don't create endless lists of product features. Instead, focus on showing the prospect how he/she will benefit from using your product.
- ✔ Make a "no-risk" offer and include a guarantee if possible.
- ✔ Make it attractive and offer a trial period or a free product sample.
- ✔ Set a deadline and make it a limited offer.
- ✔ Call to action and make it easy to reply using a toll-free number, a return envelope with pre-paid postage, a business reply card etc.
- ✔ Use a powerful PS – The abbreviation PS stands for postscript – from the Latin post (= after) scriptum (=written, writing). The recipient's eyes often move down to the bottom of the page, to the signature (Do I know the sender?) and to the PS (What is the bottom line? What does the sender want?), before they decide to read the main part of the letter. Therefore, you should summarize and restate the main advantage for the prospect in the PS.

Avoid these common faults when composing sales letters:

- Lack of targeting
- Lack of personalization
- Lack of clarity
- Lack of originality
- Lack of credibility

2 Using the AIDA formula for writing persuasive sales letters

When writing a sales letter, you should always apply the AIDA formula. The acronym AIDA stands for **A** = attention, **I** = interest, **D** = desire and **A** = action and describes a 4-stage process used for advertising.

Attention

The first step is to attract and grab the reader's attention and create awareness that your product or service is available. Start with the recipient's most pressing problem. The headline and lead paragraph must be powerful and magnetic.

Interest

Now it's time to raise the prospect's interest by providing an innovative and unique solution. Show that you understand their issues and use vital information to explain how you can help. Create more interest by focusing on advantages and benefits.

Desire

At this stage, you have to convince the reader and create an intense desire for your product. Use persuasion and emotional appeal to demonstrate how your product will satisfy the customer's needs.

Action

Now tell the prospect what he has to do next, how to get in contact with you and how to get his hands on the solution. This "call to action" is a simple statement to communicate what you want the reader to do next: make a phone call, go to your website, order a sample, sign up for the newsletter, fill in and send the reply card etc.

Key Phrases for writing sales letter

- Dear Mr Collins/Dear Sydney/Dear Reader/Dear Friend
- Are you having trouble with/getting/achieving/making ...?
- Is *[describe frequent problem]* taking up too much of your time and money?
- If you are like most business owners, you have trouble ...
- Are you tired of getting/losing/having *[the problem]?*
- When was the last time you checked to see how much your company was spending on ...?
- In fact, many businesses find that they are actually losing money.
- Who do you know that ...? Who is ...? Who does ...?
- What if ...? What is...? What do ...?
- Where do you see yourself/your company in 5 five years from now?
- How often does your ...? How often do you ...? How do you handle/manage/deal with...?
- Why is it that ...? Why do you always ...?
- Do you think ...? Do you wish ...? Do you realize that ...? Did you know that ...?
- Don't you have ...? Don't you just love the way ...? Don't you just hate the way ...?
- You don't have to be a ... You don't need to be a ... You don't need a ...
- This is why it is important to ... *[e.g. "select a company you trust"]*
- At *[our company's name]* we have the experience and the skills to help you with/getting/achieving/making ...
- Now, our professional services can handle every detail of your ... at a lower cost.
- Discover the new ... Discover the secret of ... Discover the Number One ... solution for ...
- Find out about the new ... You will love your new ...
- Just imagine ... Imagine your new ...

- Have you ever wondered why some companies/managers are more successful than others?
- Have you ever asked yourself if there is a better/easier/faster way to …?
- Save time … Save money … Save hassle … Save money and hassle with our new …
- More capacity … More flexibility … More storage … More power … More time for …
- Lower costs … Less paperwork … Fewer errors …
- ZERO downtime … ZERO waste … ZERO effort … ZERO cost … ZERO risk …
- FREE sample … FREE trial … FREE consultation … FREE upgrade … FREE delivery …
- Limited edition … Exclusive benefits …
- Only 75 left in stock … Only available for 6 weeks … Only available this week …
- This is the only product that … We are the only company that …
- Only the original … Choose the original … This is the original … Just the original …
- The safe way to … The easy way to … The safe and easy way to get instant results.
- Guaranteed results! Proven success!
- Power, Performance and Precision.
- Save time. Save money. Get instant results.
- That's what we guarantee!
- Fast! Easy! Low Cost!
- Guaranteed results! On time – every time. Or it's free!
- We can provide you a more dependable courier service at half the price you are paying now.
- What's more, there is no fee for this service. We only take a percentage of …
- Please review the list of companies that already use our products and services. Call them and ask them about our efficiency.
- When may we stop by and offer you a FREE consultation and demonstrate how much money you will save in the forthcoming weeks, months and years?
- We have a special introductory offer for you. Try our services for 6 months at half our regular price.
- To take advantage of this special price, all you have to do is return the enclosed business reply card within two weeks or call our toll-free number. After 31 March 20.. this special offer will no longer be available.
- Return the enclosed card today and receive the first issue free.
- 100 % satisfaction guaranteed! If you're not happy with …, we don't expect you to pay.
- If you are not 100 % satisfied for any reason, you may cancel your order without any hassle and still keep your gift/FREE sample.
- If you are not 100 % satisfied with your product, you can return or exchange it within 90 days from the date of purchase.
- 100 % Money-Back Guarantee! If for any reason you are not completely satisfied with your new …, you will receive a full refund.
- Give us a call and make an appointment with one of our experienced representatives.
- Call us … Call now … Call today for a free estimate/consultation/quotation/catalogue …
- Visit us online at www. … .com
- Act today and call our toll-free number or visit our website at www. … .com
- PS: Numerous satisfied customers are already saving more than 33 % of their office expenses! We can do the same for you!

3 Sample sales letter

SecuGuard Ltd

SecuGuard Ltd
37 Royal Park Rd
London NW10 7UL
www.SecuGuard.co.uk
info@SecuGuard.co.uk
telephone 0800 77 44 77
25 August 20..

Highfield Industries Ltd
28 Venice St
Manchester M1 3HB

Dear Mr Porter

Are you having trouble finding important documents when you need them?

Is organizing your paperwork taking up too much of your time?

Then we have got an important message for you! – There is a better way!

Managing your documents has never been easier! Trusted since 2004 with over 30,000 clients and 900,000 users worldwide, our web-based, document management software allows you to manage your documents more efficiently and increase office performance.

At SecuGuard Ltd we have the experience and the skills to help you organize your office data, files and documents.

Discover the number one document management solution for your company and save time, money and hassle with our new Intel DM Pro 8000. The safe and easy way to organize your office and get instant results! Guaranteed!

Just imagine how easy it would be to find any document or information you need with just a few clicks and within a matter of seconds.

Less paperwork! Zero risk! More time for important tasks!

For a limited time only, we have a special introductory offer for you. Try our additional professional support services for 3 months at half of our regular price.

And there's more! We are completely confident that you will be 100 % delighted with our software. That's why we are offering an unconditional 90-day 100 % money-back guarantee. If for any reason you are not completely satisfied, simply contact us to receive a full refund.

Act today and call our toll-free number 0800 77 44 77 for a free consultation or visit us online at www. SecuGuard.com.

Yours sincerely

Aysel Koç

Aysel Koç

Managing Director

PS: Numerous satisfied customers are already saving time and money with SecuGuard!
We can do the same for you!

Exercise – Sales letter

B1

Ihre Firma Ergo Office Design, Bahnhofstr. 82, 90443 Nürnberg, produziert innovative Regalsysteme, ergonomische Bürostühle und Schreibtische.

Verfassen Sie im Rahmen einer Direktwerbung einen Brief an das Unternehmen Crown Plaza Office Services, 64 Castle St, Liverpool L2 7LQ, Großbritannien. Nutzen Sie das Prinzip der AIDA-Formel und beschreiben Sie dabei ein typisches Problem. Sprechen Sie ggf. Schwächen anderer Produkte oder Hersteller an. Bieten Sie Lösungen und betonen Sie die Vorzüge Ihrer Produkte. Gewähren Sie eine Zufriedenheitsgarantie und bewegen Sie den Adressaten dazu, sobald wie möglich mit Ihnen Kontakt aufzunehmen.

EOD
Ergo Office Design

Exercise – Analysing the market

A2

Background

Your company is planning to launch a new colour photocopier. You are working in the market research department and your superior has asked you to find out about other colour photocopiers on sale.

Photocopier	Manufacturer	Performance*	Price in USD	Market Area	Advertised
Copy Star FC-8000	Star Copy Ltd	up to 68 ppm 50,000 cpm	$ 4,299	Europe**, UK***, USA, Canada	television, magazines
Office Line iQ 7055	iQ Office Equipment	up to 60 ppm 65,000 cpm	$ 4,385	Europe**, UK***, USA, Asia	newspapers, magazines, trade fairs
Silver Motion DX 920	New Motion Digital Technology	up to 55 ppm 25,000 cpm	$ 3,910	USA, Canada	magazines, trade fairs
Copy Jet Pro 5600	NHQ Photocopiers	up to 60 ppm 70,000 cpm	$ 4,150	Europe**, UK***	newspapers, magazines, trade fairs
Blue Bay XL 4 Colour	Blue Bay Office Solutions	up to 38 ppm 12,000 cpm	$ 3,820	Europe**, UK***, USA, Asia	sale through representatives only (no adverts)
Lexus Pro C 3200	NHQ Photocopiers	up to 70 ppm 56,000 cpm	$ 4,280	Europe**, UK***	newspapers, magazines, trade fairs
KYO Colour Series 7	KYO Enterprises	up to 47 ppm 38,000 cpm	$ 4,190	Europe**, UK***, USA, Asia	magazines, trade fairs

** Continental Europe (mainland), excluding the British Isles
*** including the Republic of Ireland (Éire)

* The abbreviation ppm stands for Pages per Minute
The abbreviation cpm stands for Copies per Month

Assignment

Look at the table and answer the questions.

1 Which company does not use advertisements?

2 Which is the fastest photocopying machine?

3 Which company does not sell its products in Europe?

4 Which is the least expensive photocopier?

5 How many companies do not present their products at trade fairs?

6 Which company offers the most expensive photocopier?

7 How many companies also cover the Canadian market?

8 Which photocopier is able to handle the largest workload?

Exercise – Scheduling advertising activities

A2

Background

Your company organizes TV advertising for a variety of companies. Your superior has left you the following message on your answering machine:

"We have just finalized the details concerning the new advertising campaign for our client Star Copy Ltd with their CEO. The new campaign will start on 1 October and there will be four different advertisements. The first and the third advert will each run for 45 seconds; the second and the fourth will run for 30 seconds each. The first two focus primarily on the company's new colour photocopier and its features and benefits. The other two commercials emphasize the unique advantages of Star Copy's additional services, e.g. maintenance, warranty etc.

'Colour up your life' is going to be the first advertisement. This will show the benefits of colour photocopies in comparison to black and white ones. The main character will be Rachel Cooper, the Canadian film star. She will also present the last advertisement 'Felina'. After 'Colour up your life' we move on to 'Feature times'. Steve Kendall presents this one. It deals with the photocopier's superior features in comparison to other devices on the market, which are offered by competitors. 'Feature times' will be shown 50 times, twice as many as the two presented by Rachel Cooper. The third in the series, 'Green light', shows the advantages of Star Copy's customer support and maintenance service, including the 5 year warranty. We've persuaded the American actor Carl Dixon to present this one. This ad will be shown twice daily for 20 days.

Beginning with 'Colour up your life', a new commercial will appear on the first of each quarter.

Please fill in the advert schedule and send it for approval to the art director."

Assignment

Complete the schedule in chronological order of appearance.

Advertisement Schedule

Title	Emphasis	Starting Date	Number of Showings	Advert Length (in seconds)	Actor/Actress

Exercise – Vocabulary Building – Idioms

B1

Learning idioms, sayings and proverbs is an excellent way to improve your fluency. Study the following idioms and use them regularly in conversation and writing. It will enrich your vocabulary, enhance your comprehension and you will be able to communicate easily and fluently with native speakers in no time.

Match the idioms with the corresponding definitions:

Idioms	Definitions
back to square one	do things strictly according to the rules
ballpark figure	get to the point, start talking about important issues
between a rock and a hard place	do or say exactly the right thing, be correct or accurate
by the book	perform numerous calculations, process loads of data
call the shots	in summary, concisely, in a brief way, using few words
crunch the numbers	start doing something too soon, act without thinking
cut corners	return to the starting point, all over again
cut to the chase	in a dilemma, faced with equally unpleasant alternatives
get someone up to speed	a rough estimate or approximate number
have your work cut out	in agreement, thinking the same way
hit the nail on the head	something easily obtained or achieved
in a nutshell	make the decisions, be in charge, tell others what to do
jump the gun	give someone all the latest information about something
learn the ropes	do something the easiest or quickest way
long shot	assign a low priority and put aside for the time being
off the top of one's head	disturb or challenge the existing
once in a blue moon	have a difficult problem or lots of work to deal with
on the same page	understand the basics of how a task or job is done
(to stay/to be) on your toes	a venture with only a very small chance of success
(to go/to be) out on a limb	develop creative, original ideas, not limited by rules
piece of cake	be ready for something to happen, be alert, be focused
put on the back burner	most important aspect of something, the final outcome
raise the bar	very rarely, almost never
rock the boat	with no previous preparation, without thinking about it
the bottom line	in a risky or vulnerable position, without support
think outside the box	set higher standards of quality, make it slightly harder

B1

Translate the following sentences into English using some of the idioms from the previous exercise.

(1) Solche Fehler passieren nur alle Jubeljahre.

___

(2) Bei diesem sehr wichtigen Projekt dürfen wir nicht pfuschen.

___

(3) Der Auftrag war ein Kinderspiel.

___

(4) Nach der Absage mussten wir wieder von vorne anfangen.

___

(5) Wir benötigen so bald wie möglich eine grobe Schätzung.

___

(6) Es ist besser, nicht für Aufruhr zu sorgen.

___

(7) Lasst uns in dieser Angelegenheit nicht überstürzt handeln.

___

(8) Mit dem Projekt wirst du alle Hände voll zu tun haben.

___

(9) Geschäftsführung und Mitarbeiter waren sich einig.

___

(10) Wir sollten keine Zeit verschwenden und es auf den Punkt bringen.

___

(11) Der neue Abteilungsleiter muss sich noch einarbeiten.

___

(12) Um Erfolg zu haben, dürfen wir nicht in Schema F denken.

___

(13) Das Unternehmen steckte in der Zwickmühle.

___

(14) Wir müssen das Projekt vorerst auf Eis legen.

___

(15) Er brachte sich in eine prekäre Lage, um seinem Kollegen zu helfen.

___

Exercise – Vocabulary Building – Phrasal Verbs about JOBS

B1 B2

Phrasal verbs are a combination of a verb and a preposition or an adverb. They are an essential part of the English language and are commonly used by native speakers. Phrasal verbs are extremely important for fluency when learning English and will greatly improve your understanding and vocabulary skills to communicate effectively. Note that each phrasal verb can have multiple different meanings.

Choose the matching verb and preposition for each definition:

________________	= employ, hire	________________	= substitute, temp*
________________	= dismiss, fire, sack	________________	= substitute, temp**
________________	= resign, quit	________________	= make an appearance, arrive, come*
________________	= do and complete a task	________________	= make an appearance, arrive, come**
________________	= not go to work, being absent	________________	= tell someone about an idea or plan to get their opinion or approval

carry | fill | lay | run | show | stand | step | take | take | turn

by | down | in for | in for | off | off | on | out | up | up

Fill in the correct phrasal verb for each sentence. Remember to adapt the tense of the verb when necessary.

(1) For this position you'll have to ________________ a number of administrative duties.

(2) We waited for quite some time, but he didn't ________________.

(3) I had to stand in for her on Tuesday when she didn't ________________.

(4) Factories are warning that they may have to ________________ workers.

(5) Can you ____________________ me at the meeting while I'm away?

(6) I'll ____________________ you while you go and get a cup of coffee.

(7) You'd better __________ that idea __________ your manager first.

(8) These days employers are ___________________ less people.

(9) The vice president ___________________ last month.

(10) I won't be in tomorrow as I'm ____________ the day _________.

1 Telephoning

In today's business world it is likely that you will have phone contact with English speaking customers and suppliers. Telephone calls in a foreign language are less daunting if you try to relax – so don't panic! Always remember, the person you are speaking to will understand that your English is not word perfect. They probably deal with other people who are not native speakers all the time. It is also safe to assume that they cannot speak all languages.

When making these calls, think about what you want to say and why you are calling. Make notes before the call, with references to the intended conversation. It is advisable to look up any vocabulary you will need during the conversation. Learn the typical key phrases and when to use them in the conversation.

It is important to speak clearly and be articulate. State who you are and the reason why you are calling, e.g. "This is … I am calling about …". When talking to native speakers it is natural for them to speak at a normal speed. However, this may prove too fast for you. Control the call by asking them to repeat what they have said, asking them to speak more slowly, and to spell words you are not familiar with. If you don't know the English alphabet, you'll have to learn it. By asking these things you will avoid any misunderstandings, which, of course, neither of you want. Confirm important details immediately, especially any dates or addresses given. Listen carefully to the phrases and vocabulary that are being used. It is likely you will be able to use the same phrases later in the conversation again. This shows the other person that you are listening to what they are saying and they, in turn, will make more of an effort to help you understand. It also creates a positive atmosphere which is important to the impression you leave.

Begin and end your call politely and don't forget to thank them for their help.

A2

Translate the following tips for leaving messages on answering machines.

✔ State the purpose or subject right away.

____

✔ Make clear who is calling by giving your full name, company, and position.

____

✔ Always give the date, time and day of the week.

____

✔ Give your phone number clearly, and then repeat it slowly, so the other person is not forced to listen to the whole message again.

____

____

✔ Leave detailed messages so that a response isn't always necessary.

____

✔ Don't forget to thank the other person at the end of your message.

____

✔ Never delete a message until you have successfully returned the person's call.

____

Key vocabulary

to return a call	zurückrufen	extension	Durchwahl
in charge of	verantwortlich für	engaged, busy	besetzt
responsible for	verantwortlich für	Hold on, please.	Bitte warten Sie.
to deal with	sich kümmern um	Hold the line, please.	Bleiben Sie bitte am Apparat.
again	wieder, noch einmal	to take a message	eine Nachricht entgegennehmen
to repeat	wiederholen	to spell	buchstabieren
I didn't catch that.	Das habe ich nicht verstanden.	to reach	erreichen
to speak up	lauter sprechen	to get hold of	erreichen
to dial a number	eine Nummer wählen	You're welcome.	Gern geschehen.
to put through	durchstellen, verbinden		
available	verfügbar		
reply	Antwort		

Key Phrases for telephone calls

Ein Gespräch entgegennehmen (Answering the phone)

- Good morning/Good afternoon, ... speaking.
- This is ... speaking.
- Who's speaking, please?/Who is calling, please?
- Who would you like to talk to, sir/madam?
- How can I help you?

Nach jemandem fragen (Asking for someone)

- Good morning, this is ... calling from ...
- I'm calling about ...
- I am returning your call.
- I'd like to speak to ..., please.
- Could you put me through to ..., please?
- Could I speak to someone who is in charge of ..., please?
- Could I speak to someone who is responsible for ..., please?
- Could I speak to someone who deals with ..., please?
- Am I speaking with ...?

Schwierigkeiten (Difficulties)

- Say again, please.
- Could you repeat the address, please?
- Could you give me the address again, please?
- Sorry, I didn't catch that.
- I can't hear you very well.
- Could you speak up, please?
- I'm sorry, but you must have dialled the wrong number.
- The line is really bad.
- Sorry, this is a really bad line.

Den Anrufer verbinden (Putting the caller through)

- I'll put you through to …
- I'll put … on the line.
- One moment please, I'll see if … is available.
- I'm sorry, there's no reply from …
- Just a moment, please. I'll put you through.
- I'm sorry, the line is engaged.
- I've tried to get through several times, but it's always engaged.
- I'm afraid he's away on business.

Den Anrufer bitten zu warten (Putting the caller on hold)

- Just a moment, please.
- Hold on, please.
- Hold the line, please.

Den Anrufer bitten, noch einmal anzurufen (Asking someone to call back)

- I'm sorry, … is in a meeting.
- I'm afraid she's not in the office today.
- Could you call back later in the day?
- Would you like to call back later?

Eine Nachricht entgegennehmen (Taking a message)

- Can I take a message?/Can I give him/her a message?
- Would you like to leave a message?
- Can I take your details?
- I'll tell him that you've called./I'll give her the message as soon as possible.
- I'll make sure he calls you back as soon as possible.
- Can she call you back when she gets in?
- Could you spell that, please?
- What was your name again, please?
- At what number can you be reached?
- When would be the best time to reach you?/When is the best time to call you back?
- When would be the best time to get hold of him?

Eine Nachricht hinterlassen (Leaving a message)

- I'd like to leave a message for …
- Could you ask him to call me back later/tomorrow/in the afternoon?

Das Gespräch beenden (Ending the call)

- Thank you for your help.
- Thank you very much. Goodbye.
- Thanks a lot. Bye.
- Bye now./Bye for now./Speak to you then.
- You're welcome. Goodbye.

Exercise – Phone calls

B1

(1) Guten Morgen. Hier spricht ... Wie kann ich Ihnen helfen?

____

(2) Wer spricht dort bitte?

____

(3) Mit wem möchten Sie sprechen?

____

(4) Ich rufe an bezüglich ...

____

(5) Könnte ich bitte mit ... sprechen?

____

(6) Ich möchte mit jemandem sprechen, der für ... zuständig ist.

____

(7) Spreche ich mit ...?

____

(8) Es tut mir leid, aber das habe ich gerade nicht verstanden.

____

(9) Könnten Sie das bitte noch einmal wiederholen?

____

(10) Wie lautet noch einmal die Adresse?

____

(11) Könnten Sie das bitte buchstabieren?

____

(12) Einen Moment bitte. Ich hole mir eben einen Kugelschreiber.

____

(13) Die Verbindung ist wirklich schlecht. Könnten Sie bitte etwas lauter sprechen?

____

(14) Tut mir leid, aber die Verbindung war plötzlich weg. Ich weiß nicht, was da passiert ist.

____

(15) Es tut mir leid, aber da müssen Sie sich wohl verwählt haben.

____

(16) Einen Moment bitte. Bitte bleiben Sie am Apparat. Ich stelle Sie durch.

____

(17) Es tut mir leid, aber sie ist nicht im Büro. Sie wird übermorgen wieder da sein.

____

(18) Es ist leider besetzt. Und sein Kollege macht gerade Mittagspause.

____

(19) Wie war noch einmal Ihr Name?

____

(20) Möchten Sie eine Nachricht hinterlassen?

____

(21) Oder möchten Sie morgen noch einmal anrufen? Vielleicht am späten Nachmittag?

____

(22) Möchten Sie die Durchwahl, um es später selber noch einmal zu versuchen?

____

(23) Soll sie Sie zurückrufen?

____

(24) Unter welcher Telefonnummer können wir Sie erreichen?

____

(25) Wann können wir Sie am besten erreichen?

____

(26) Das ist schade. Es ist eigentlich ziemlich dringend.

____

(27) Sagen Sie ihm bitte, dass ich morgen Vormittag noch einmal anrufen werde.

____

(28) Ich werde ihr die Nachricht umgehend geben und sicherstellen, dass sie Sie so bald wie möglich zurückruft.

____

(29) Vielen Dank für Ihre Hilfe.

____

(30) Gern geschehen. Auf Wiederhören. Und grüßen Sie bitte Gary von mir.

____

Exercise – Vocabulary Building – Phrasal Verbs for TELEPHONING

B1 B2

Phrasal verbs are a combination of a verb and a preposition or an adverb. They are an essential part of the English language and are commonly used by native speakers. Phrasal verbs are extremely important for fluency when learning English and will greatly improve your understanding and vocabulary skills to communicate effectively. Note that each phrasal verb can have multiple different meanings.

Choose the matching verb and preposition for each definition:

____________	= reach sb. on the phone	____________	= end a telephone call
____________	= connect sb. with sb.	____________	= wait for a short time (informal)
____________	= speak louder	____________	= wait for a short time
____________	= telephone so. later (again)	____________	= interrupted telephone call
____________	= finish talking on the phone	____________	= become inaudible (because of a bad connection)

break – cut – get – get – get – hang – hang – hold – put – speak

back – on – on – off – off – up – up – up – through – through

Fill in the appropriate phrasal verb for each sentence. Remember to adapt the tense of the verb when necessary.

(1) ____________ – there's something else I need to tell you.

(2) I finally ____________ to the department.

(3) Could you ____________ for a moment, please?

(4) This is a really bad line. Could you ____________, please?

(5) I have no idea what happened. We got ____________ in the middle of our conversation.

(6) Could you ________ me ________ to the sales department, please?

(7) I'll find out and ____________ to you as soon as possible.

(8) I just ____________ the phone with the managing director. I'll fill you in on.

(9) After I ____________ I remembered what I'd wanted to say.

(10) Could you repeat that, please? I can hardly hear you. You're ____________.

Exercise – Organizing annual leave

A2

Background

You work in the personnel department and are responsible for organizing annual leave in your branch. Your superior, Jane Bristow, has left you the following message on your voicemail:

"Allison is merely taking the last week in June. She originally planned for a longer holiday this summer, but changed her mind and is now taking most of it at the end of the year. Eric is taking the first three weeks in June. Steven's taking the entire June and the first week of July, as he has lots of days left and booked a holiday with his family. Mary would like to take two weeks from 11 July and an additional week in the middle of August, as she will get a visit from her family on 17 August for a couple of days. John has asked for the first three weeks in August, but this won't work, as he must be back in time to prepare the upcoming trade fair. Sign him in for the first two weeks of the month instead. Ted would like the second half of August. That should work out alright. William doesn't really mind when to take his leave. The last week of July and the following week should be fine. And I'll be taking a fortnight from 13 June. I'll might take another week at the end of August, but I can't tell yet."

Assignment

Complete the schedule below by marking the annual leave with a cross (X).

Annual Leave Booking													
Month	**June** (week beginning on …)				**July** (week beginning on …)				**August** (week beginning on …)				
Employee	6	13	20	27	4	11	18	25	1	8	15	22	29
Jane Bristow													
John Carter													
Steven Foster													
William Gibson													
Mary Lynch													
Allison Miller													
Ted Murphy													
Eric Peters													

Exercise – Scheduling job interviews

A2

Background

You work in the human resources department of a local company. You are discussing the current job applications with your colleague Jennifer.

You: I can see you have the new applications.

Jennifer: Yes, just reading them through.

You: Are you planning to interview next week?

Jennifer: Yes, I have arranged them for Wednesday.

You: Can you do all the interviews on your own, or do you need me?

Jennifer: I think I'll take the first four, starting at 9 am. Could you do the last two? I'd really appreciate your help.

You: Sure, anytime.

Jennifer: If we allow half an hour each and break for coffee after the third interview for quarter of an hour, we should finish before lunch.

You: Do you want to go over them again?

Jennifer: Yes, good idea. Well, we have John O'Shea and Amy Cooper. Both sound suitable for the job and they are both the same age, 25. And then there's another woman. She is two years younger than them.

You: Can I see?

Jennifer: Of course. Here you are. Ann Caffrey, she is currently with OfficeWorks together with John O'Shea.

You: Who else do we have?

Jennifer: There are Maureen Sullivan and Michael Casey, both work at Parker Smyth. Michael is 21. Maureen is actually five years older than him.
And finally there's Mary O'Donovan who is 22. She is presently without a job.

You: I will arrange the interviews in alphabetical order, using the surnames, if that's okay with you.

Jennifer: Certainly, that's fine. Wait ... Michael doesn't work for Parker Smyth anymore. He's now with TrendLine. How could I forget ... he sent me an email last week.

You: Where does Amy Cooper work?

Jennifer: She used to work at OfficeWorks but is now with Giles.

Assignment

Use the information from the conversation to fill in the interview schedule.

Applicant's Name	Age	Present Employer	Starting Time

Exercise – Arranging an interview

B1

Background

Sie haben den Zeitplan für die Interviews erstellt und müssen nun die Bewerber zum Vorstellungsgespräch einladen.

Assignment

Schreiben Sie eine E-Mail an die Kandidatin Amy Cooper (amy.cooper@webmail.com) und laden Sie die Bewerberin zu einem Vorstellungsgespräch am Mittwoch, dem 18. Juni 20.. um 10.00 Uhr ein.

Bitten Sie Frau Cooper, alle relevanten Zertifikate und einen aktuellen Lebenslauf mitzubringen.

Teilen Sie der Bewerberin mit, dass das Vorstellungsgespräch ungefähr eine halbe Stunde dauern und im Raum N02 im zweiten Stock stattfinden wird, sie sich aber zuerst an der Rezeption im Erdgeschoss melden soll.

Kostenlose Parkplätze befinden sich im Parkhaus gegenüber dem Firmengebäude.

Schicken Sie darüber hinaus eine Kopie der E-Mail an Ihre Kollegin Jennifer Parker (jennifer.parker@bewleys-dublin.ie).

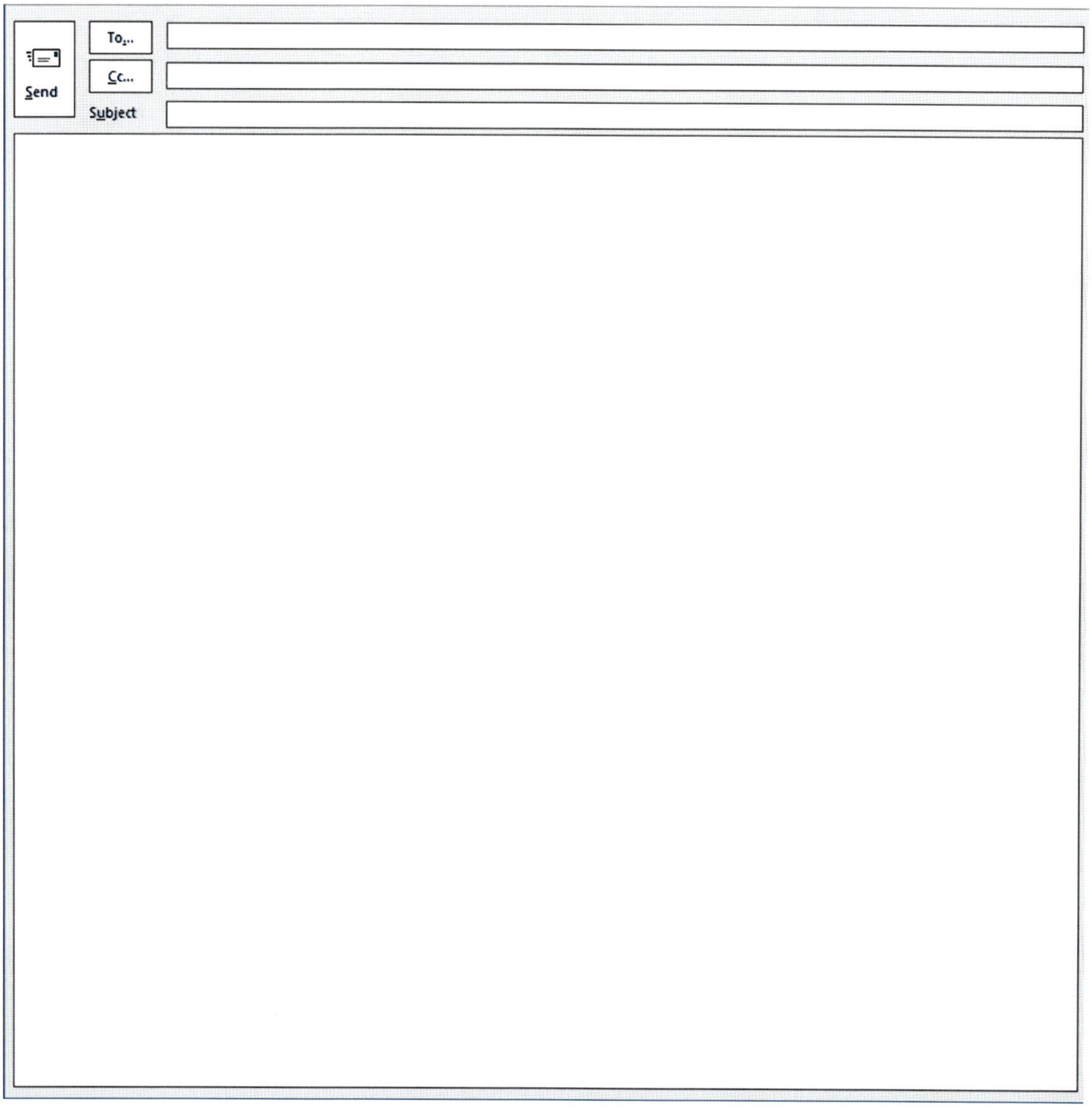

Exercise – Deciding on a suitable employee to hire

A2

Background

You work in the personnel department of a multinational company, which needs to hire a qualified interpreter and translator to participate in business negotiations and deal with enquiries from abroad.

Name	Age	Languages spoken	University attended	Years of Experience	Salary (£)	Male or Female
Luisa Ferrara	41	Dutch, French, German, Italian, Portuguese, Spanish	University of Milan, Italy	12	48,000	female
Pawel Nowak	52	Czech, Greek, Polish, Russian	Charles University Prague, Czech Republic	23	57,000	male
Safiea Ansary	39	Hindi, Pashto, Persian, Urdu	Kabul University, Afghanistan	13	62,000	female
Berat Miraç	33	Arabic, Chinese, German, Hebrew, Persian, Turkish	Umm Al-Qura University, Makkah, Saudi Arabia	8	89,000	male
Mai-Lin Zhao Yang	45	Chinese, Japanese, Korean, Taiwanese, Vietnamese	Shanghai University, China	15	76,000	female

Assignment

Look at the table of candidates and answer the questions.

1 How many candidate are able to speak German?

2 How many candidates speak more than four languages?

3 How many different languages are listed in the table?

4 Which candidate offers the most years of experience?

5 Which female candidate has the least experience?

6 At which university did the youngest female candidate study?

7 How many years of experience has the candidate with the lowest salary?

8 Which candidate receives the highest salary?

9 How many languages does Luisa Ferrara speak?

10 How many candidates have more than twelve years of experience?

11 Which candidate is able to speak Urdu?

12 How many candidates attended a European university?

Exercise – Managing performance records

B1

Background

Your firm organizes computer training seminars for employees of other companies. A group of 8 participants has just finished a 2-week course on office applications.

Your colleague has left you the following message on your voicemail:

"All of them have finally finished their examinations. Well, Patrick didn't turn up for his spreadsheet exam, but that wasn't really a surprise after he failed both of the other exams, word processing and presentations.

Brian Gallagher wasn't bad either. Just missed a distinction in data base but got it in both, word processing and presentations.

Mary Burke did two, word processing and spreadsheets, and passed both with credit.

Pat was the most successful candidate which ITS Ltd has ever sent. Three distinctions and a credit in data base; she's really excellent. She didn't take the word processing exam, as she got that the last time she was here.

Fiona Doyle just took the word processing. And passed, of course.

Ted O'Neill tried the data base, but he failed. Well, it is after all the most difficult exam.

Maureen O'Brien tried it as well, and didn't make it either. But she got a credit in the internet one and even a distinction with the presentations.

Mike was quite good, I suppose. Got a credit in presentations, but missed the distinction with the word processing and just managed to get through the spreadsheets.

So we had 20 exams in total, didn't we?"

Assignment

You are responsible for maintaining the training records. Use the information from the memo to complete the following training report.

TRAINING REPORT

Company ______________________________

Course Title ______________________________

Course Length ______________________________

D = Dinstinction
C = Credit
P = Pass
F = Fail
A = Absent

Canditates	Modules: WORD PROCESSING	SPREADSHEET CALCULATION	DATA BASE	PRESENTATIONS	INTERNET AND EMAIL	Exam Results
Michael O'Donnell						
Ted O'Neill						
Maureen O'Brien						
Mary Burke						
Patricia O'Leary						
Patrick O'Carroll						
Brian Gallagher						
Fiona Doyle						

Exercise – Vocabulary Building – Phrasal Verbs about MONEY

B1 B2

Phrasal verbs are a combination of a verb and a preposition or an adverb. They are an essential part of the English language and are commonly used by native speakers. Phrasal verbs are extremely important for fluency when learning English and will greatly improve your understanding and vocabulary skills to communicate effectively. Note that each phrasal verb can have multiple different meanings.

Choose the matching verb and preposition for each definition:

________________	= finish paying money owed	________________	= reduce the money which is spent
________________	= allow a debt to increase	________________	= save money for a particular purpose
________________	= pay a part of money you owe	________________	= gradually increase the amount
________________	= make or earn money	________________	= inherit money when s.o. dies
________________	= arrange to get a bank loan	________________	= have enough money for the basics

bring | build | come | cut | live | pay | put | set/put | run | take

aside | back on | down | in | into | off | on | out | up | up

Fill in the correct phrasal verb for each sentence. Remember to adapt the tense of the verb when necessary.

(1) We have to finance the project and must consider how we can ________ funds _____.

(2) The company must ________ its cash reserves _____ to a sufficient level.

(3) He ________________ a small fortune when his uncle died.

(4) We must ________________ expenditure in order to remain solvent.

(5) He has barely enough money to ________________.

(6) They ________________ their mortgage after twenty years.

(7) We had to __________ a 10 % deposit ________ to the secure the offer.

(8) You should try to ________ some money ________ in case of emergencies.

(9) The company has ________________ a deficit of £40,000.

(10) They ________________ a loan to purchase the delivery van.

Exercise – Vocabulary Building – Phrasal Verbs about PROBLEMS

B1 B2

Phrasal verbs are a combination of a verb and a preposition or an adverb. They are an essential part of the English language and are commonly used by native speakers. Phrasal verbs are extremely important for fluency when learning English and will greatly improve your understanding and vocabulary skills to communicate effectively. Note that each phrasal verb can have multiple different meanings.

Choose the matching verb and preposition for each definition:

________________	= seek and find a solution	________________	= tolerate or endure an issue
________________	= take action to handle a problem	________________	= circumvent, avoid, evade
________________	= come across difficulties	________________	= hide, conceal
________________	= suggest or think of an idea or plan	________________	= make a great effort, fight
________________	= wait without taking action until an unpleasant situation is over	________________	= reduce the number of possibilities

come · cover · deal · figure · get · narrow · put · run · sit · struggle

down · with · with · into · out · out · round/around · up · up with · up with

Fill in the correct phrasal verb for each sentence. Remember to adapt the tense of the verb when necessary.

(1) They tried to ________________ the matter by lying, but in vain.

(2) I didn't know what the problem was, but I finally ______________ it __________.

(3) There's no solution. We have to ________________ the situation for the time being.

(4) The event was going well. However, at the last moment we ______________ problems.

(5) We have to ________________ a better solution.

(6) Remember the proverb "Let sleeping dogs lie". Let's wait and _______ it ______.

(7) Let's see if we can ________________ the number of possible causes.

(8) He ________________ the problem by an ingenious trick.

(9) How do you intend to ________________ this problem?

(10) It was a tough problem. He ____________________ the issue for hours.

Exercise – At the Airport

A2

Do you know what the following signs mean?

____

____

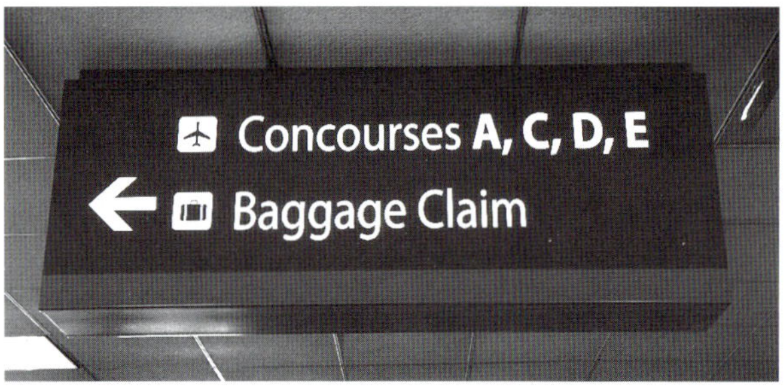

____

____

____

____

Do you know what the following signs mean?

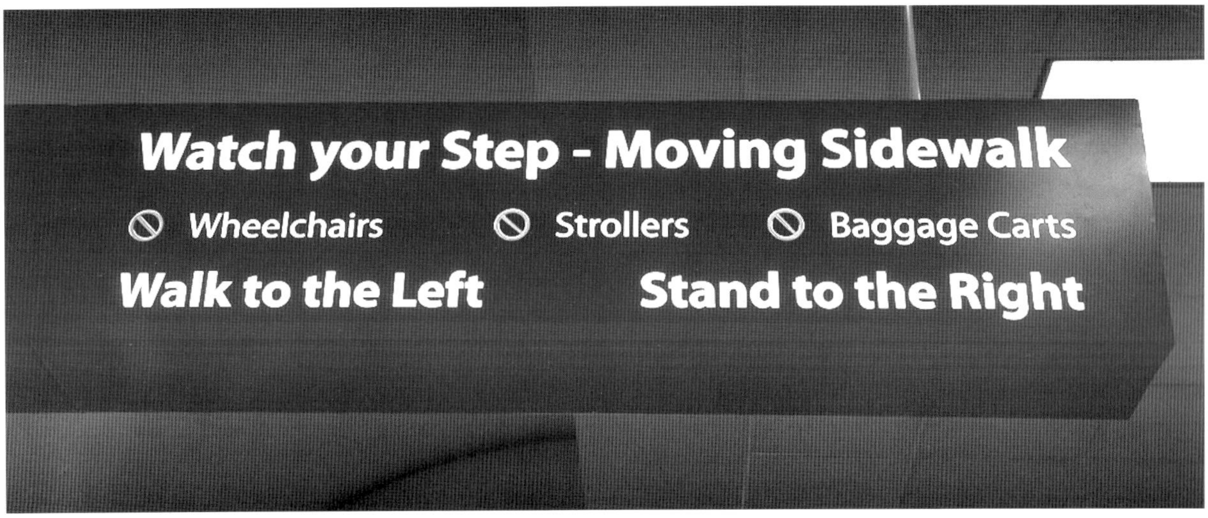

Exercise – Arranging hotel reservations

A2

Background

You work in the office of a consulting firm and are responsible for hotel reservations.

You have received the following message on your voicemail:

"Kate is looking into things at ITC Ltd in Galway. Steve needs to stay for a night at Benner's in Limerick. He is paying OfficeLine a short visit, first thing on the 8th. DataTec has specifically asked for Declan. He must have left a good impression the last time he was there. He will stay at the Brandon in Tralee. John will need 5 days at Bewley's in Dublin. He would like to stay the four nights at the Oakpark Inn. He has to leave again on the 26th as he has an assignment in Cork on the 27th. Kate has to be there by the 17th. I suppose she'll need 3 nights, so book her into Horan's. Declan wants to get there on the 4th, but he reckons that 2 nights will do."

Assignment

Complete the table and list the companies in alphabetical order.

Hotel Reservations

Company	Town	Hotel	Arrival	Departure	Consultant

Exercise – Booking a hotel room

A2

Background

Sie haben die Planung abgeschlossenen und nehmen gegenwärtig die Hotelbuchungen vor.

Assignment

Schreiben Sie eine E-Mail an das Oakpark Inn Hotel (bookings@oakpark-inn.ie) und buchen Sie ein Zimmer für John O'Sullivan vom 22. bis zum 26. des Monats.

Teilen Sie dem Hotel mit, dass John morgens früh um 8:30 Uhr einchecken muss, da er bereits um 10:30 Uhr einen Termin beim Kunden hat.

Darüber hinaus benötigt John einen Mietwagen, welcher vom Hotel organisiert werden soll.

Die Rechnung soll wie immer an das Unternehmen geschickt werden. Für die Unterkunft soll der übliche Firmenkundenrabatt gewährt werden.

Bitten Sie um eine Bestätigung per Fax.

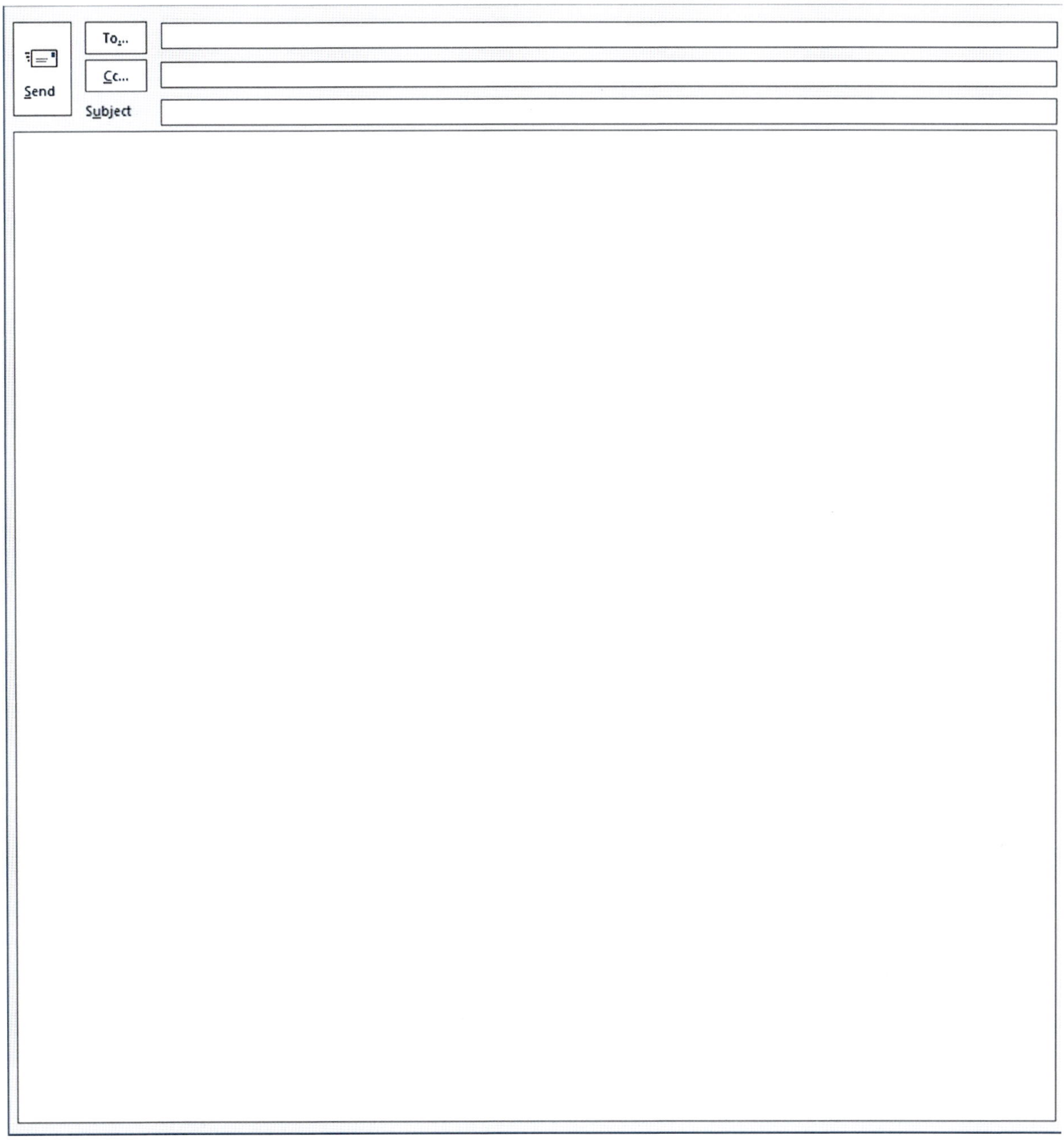

Exercise – Making a reservation

A2

Background

A colleague of yours, Azra Melek, who is currently on business in Ireland, has to visit a number of customers in Limerick.

She has sent you the following note:

SOUTHBRIDGE INVESTMENTS PLC

12 Kingsway

London WC2B 6XF

Phone: 020 7648 7410

Fax: 020 7648 7490

Email: enquiries@southbridge.co.uk

Hi!

I'm almost finished in Dublin and have to go on to Limerick now.

Book me into the Grandeur – a single room with bath and shower.

I'll get there at about 7 o'clock in the evening on the 21st.

I'll be staying for two nights and I'll need wireless internet access and ask them to organize a rental car.

Their fax number is 00353 61 377 855.

Thanks

Azra

Assignment

Use the note to fill in the hotel booking form for your colleague.

Hotel Booking Form

COMPLETE IN BLOCK CAPITALS

Hotel ____________________ **Fax** ____________________

Town ____________________

Name ____________________

Company ____________________

Address ____________________

____

Telephone ____________________

☐ single room

☐ double room

☐ twin-bedded room

(Please tick)

Check-in ____________________

Check-out ____________________

Other requirements:

____

____

____

Date ____________________

Signature ____________________

Exercise – Organizing events

A2

Background

You are employed at the London City Conference Centre. During the planning meeting with your manager, Aaron Banks, arrangements are being made for the reservations.

We are fully booked on 25 August 20.. This morning, Saray Apparel phoned to reserve the Riverside suite for their fashion show. Irish Crystal would like the Sky Lodge suite. Bill should take that one. They are launching their new range. It will start at 2 o'clock. Kelly's Bakery are having their AGM in the Grand Tower suite. It begins at 10 am. They wanted the Rooftop suite, but Tara Books has reserved it for a press reception. Jessica hasn't done a press reception yet, has she? It'll be a good experience for her. As they don't start till 9 o'clock, we have ample time to prepare the rooms. Mark can look after Saray Apparel and Kelly's Bakery. Saray Apparel starts at 1630 hrs.

Assignment

Complete the schedule and list the customers in alphabetical order.

Bookings for 25 August 20..

Customer	Event	Suite	Staff	Time

Exercise – Vocabulary Building – Prepositions (1)

B1

Prepositions are an important part of the English language. They are used to indicate a relationship between a noun or pronoun in a sentence and another word in the sentence.

Fill in the correct preposition for each sentence.

(1) I'll see you ______________ the conference.

(2) ______________ the time I arrived, the train had already left.

(3) The elevator was ______________ order.

(4) When ______________ doubt, please look the address up in the personnel file.

(5) We had Wi-Fi in all the hotels we stayed ______________.

(6) There is an island just about four miles ______________ the coast.

(7) She's ______________ leave until the end of the month.

(8) We'd like to have a room with a view ______________ the sea.

(9) The fire was now ______________ control.

(10) He was able to describe the accident ______________ detail.

(11) The products are ______________ sale at the moment.

(12) We have to be there ______________ 4 p.m. at the latest. Otherwise, they won't let us in.

(13) It sounds great ______________ theory, but will your plan work?

(14) He started learning Chinese ______________ the age of 10.

(15) I don't know ______________ certain, but I think he's off today.

(16) He's currently abroad ______________ business.

(17) The data on thumb drive were gone, so we had to start ______________ scratch.

(18) I ran ______________ my old colleague the other day.

(19) The unexpected visit took us ______________ surprise.

(20) His train arrived ______________ time.

at	at	at	by	by	by	for	from	in	in
in	into	of	off	on	on	on	on	out of	out of

Exercise – Vocabulary Building – Prepositions (2)

B1

Prepositions are an important part of the English language. They are used to indicate a relationship between a noun or pronoun in a sentence and another word in the sentence.

Fill in the correct preposition for each sentence.

(1) What are you talking ______________?

(2) She studied business management ______________ university.

(3) I'm sorry. I must have done it ______________ mistake.

(4) Ben is responsible ______________ managing the entire project.

(5) He came to work ______________ Wednesday, but didn't show up on Thursday.

(6) They've just arrived and will be ______________ you in a minute.

(7) She waved us good-bye until our car was ______________ sight.

(8) Our contracts are currently ______________ review.

(9) He reminds me ______________ my old mathematics teacher.

(10) It's ______________ time you told him the truth.

(11) I have to apologize ______________ being late.

(12) The manager didn't take part ______________ the discussion.

(13) He's rather good ______________ accounting.

(14) We arrived at the airport just ______________ time to catch the plane.

(15) This is my first visit ______________ China.

(16) Traffic will be diverted while the road is ______________ repair.

(17) The rule is that someone must be ______________ duty at all times.

(18) Mark has a reputation ______________ being late all the time.

(19) She deleted the files by accident. She didn't do it ______________ purpose.

(20) Don't worry ______________ it. Everything will be fine.

at	at	about	about	about	by	for	for	for	in
in	of	on	on	on	out of	to	under	under	with

Alphabetical wordlist

a variety of	eine Vielzahl an
abbreviation	Abkürzung
above date	oben genanntes Datum
absent	abwesend
abstentions	Enthaltungen
abstract	Kurzbeschreibung, Abriss
accept (verb)	annehmen, akzeptieren
acceptance	Annahme, Zustimmung
access	Zugriff, Zugang, Zutritt
accommodate (verb)	aufnehmen, unterbringen
accommodation	Unterkunft, Unterbringung
according to	gemäß, entsprechend, mit Bezug auf
account	Konto
accounting	Buchhaltung, Buchführung, Rechnungswesen
achieved	erreicht
acknowledge (verb)	bestätigen
acknowledgement	Bestätigung
acronym	Initialwort, Akronym
action	Handlung
actually	eigentlich
adapted	angepasst, bearbeitet, eingerichtet, umgestellt
address (verb)	ansprechen
adjourn (verb)	vertagen, aussetzen, beenden
adjourned	vertagt, beendet
adjusted	eingestellt, angepasst, korrigiert
adjustment	Anpassung
administration	Verwaltung, Organisation
advance payment	Vorkasse, Vorauszahlung
advanced	fortschrittlich, weitentwickelt, anspruchsvoll
advantage	Vorteil
advertisement	Werbeanzeige
advertising	Werbung
advertising calls	Vertreterbesuche
advisable	ratsam
advise about/of (verb)	informieren, mitteilen
advised	empfohlen, angeraten
aerospace and aviation	Luft- und Raumfahrt
affairs	Angelegenheiten
affiliate	Tochterunternehmen
again	wieder, noch einmal
age	Alter
agenda	Tagesordnung
agreed	vereinbart, abgesprochen
agreement	Vereinbarung, Einverständnis, Zustimmung
agriculture	Landwirtschaft
ahead	im Voraus
aimless	ziellos, planlos
air waybill	Luftfrachtbrief
allow (verb)	gewähren, gestatten
allocate	zuteilen
already	bereits, schon
alter (verb)	ändern, modifizieren
amended	ergänzt, geändert, berichtigt
amenities	Annehmlichkeiten
amount	Betrag
ample	reichlich, genügend
and so on	und so weiter
and the like	und so weiter
announce (verb)	ankündigen, mitteilen, bekannt geben, verkünden
annual leave	Jahresurlaub
answering machine	Anrufbeantworter
any	jegliches, jedes, alle, irgendein
any other business	Tagesordnungspunkt „Sonstiges"
apology	Entschuldigung
apologize (verb)	sich entschuldigen
apparel	Bekleidung
appear (verb)	erscheinen, auftreten, sichtbar werden
appendix	Anhang
applicant	Bewerber
application	Anwendung
apply (verb)	anwenden, Anwendung finden
appointment	Termin
appreciate (verb)	schätzen, würdigen
approach (verb)	Kontakt aufnehmen
appropriate	passend, geeignet
approval	Zustimmung, Genehmigung, Billigung
approximately	ungefähr, circa, schätzungsweise
app	Anwendung
archival storage	Archivierung
area	Bereich, Gebiet
arise (verb)	auftreten, sich ergeben, entstehen
arrangements	Maßnahmen, Vorbereitungen
arrival	Ankunft
articulate	deutlich, gut verständlich
as agreed	wie vereinbart
as soon as	sobald wie
as stated	wie angegeben
ascend (verb)	ansteigen
ascertain (verb)	ermitteln, feststellen, erfragen, erkunden, herausfinden
assets	Aktiva, Vermögensgegenstände
assign (verb)	(eine Aufgabe) zuweisen, zuordnen
assignment	Aufgabe
assume (verb)	annehmen
at short notice	kurzfristig
at the latest	spätestens
at this stage	zu diesem Zeitpunkt
at your expense	auf Ihre Kosten
ATM (automated teller machine)	Geldautomat
attach (verb)	anhängen, anheften
attachment	Anhang
attend (verb)	teilnehmen
attendance	Anwesenheit, Teilnahme
attendee	Anwesend, Teilnehmer, Besucher
attention	Aufmerksamkeit
attract (verb)	anlocken, anziehen, ansprechen, werben
audience	Zielgruppe, Empfänger, Publikum
audit	Prüfung, Betriebsprüfung
automotive technology	Automobiltechnologie
availability	Verfügbarkeit, Lieferbarkeit
available	verfügbar, erhältlich
aviation	Luftfahrt
avoid (verb)	vermeiden
awards	Preisverleihung, Auszeichnungen
awareness	Bewusstsein
baggage cart	Gepäckwagen
baggage claim	Gepäckausgabe
balance	Saldo, Differenz
balance sheet	Bilanz
based	basierend, basiert
based in	mit Sitz in, gelegen, befindlich
basic	einfach, elementar, grundlegend, regulär
be addressed (verb)	sollen angesprochen werden
be aware of (verb)	sich bewusst sein
be based on (verb)	basieren auf
be familiar with (verb)	vertraut mit
be tired of (verb)	es leid sein, es satt haben
become (verb)	werden
beneath	unterhalb

benefit from (verb)	profitieren, nutzen ziehen von
benefits	Nutzen
besides	außerdem, abgesehen von, obendrein, überdies
beverage	Getränk
bidding	Ausschreibungsverfahren
bill of exchange (B/E)	Wechsel
bill of lading (B/L)	Konnossement, Seefrachtbrief, Ladeschein
body (letter)	Hauptteil (Brief); Körper
boost (verb)	steigern, stärken, fördern
bottleneck	Engpass
bottom	unteres Ende, Unterteil
bottom line	Endresultat, Quintessenz, Schlussfolgerung, Reingewinn
bouquet of flowers	Blumenstrauß
branch	Filiale, Zweigstelle
brand	Warenzeichen, Marke
breakdown	Betriebsstörung, Ausfall
break-even-point	Gewinnschwelle
brief	kurz
briefcase	Aktentasche
brochure	Broschüre
building blocks	Bausteine
bulk orders	Großaufträge
bulky	sperrig, voluminös
business associate	Geschäftspartner
business owner	Inhaber, Eigentümer
business reply card	Rückantwortkarte
business transaction	Geschäftsabwicklung
business world	Geschäftswelt
cable	Kabel
call it a day (verb)	beenden, es bei etw. belassen
call to action	Handlungsaufforderung
call to order	Eröffnung (einer Konferenz oder Sitzung)
cancel (verb)	stornieren
capable	fähig, imstande
capacity	Fassungsvermögen, Kapazität
capture (verb)	erfassen, erobern
case	Fall, Angelegenheit, Sache, Kiste, Gehäuse
cash discount	Skonto
cash in advance	Vorkasse, Vorauszahlung
cash on delivery	Zahlung bei Lieferung, gegen Nachnahme
cash with order	Zahlung bei Auftragserteilung
casual	zwanglos, ungezwungen, leger, lässig
catalogue	Katalog
category	Kategorie, Rubrik
century	Jahrhundert
certificate	Zertifikat
certificate of origin	Ursprungszeugnis
chairman	Vorsitzender, Vorstand
chamber of commerce and industry	Industrie- und Handelskammer
chance	Gelegenheit, Chance, Möglichkeit
characteristics	Eigenschaften
charge	Gebühr, Preis
chemistry	Chemie
child care	Kinderbetreuung, Kinderpflege
choice	Wahl
choices	Wahlmöglichkeiten
circulate (verb)	verteilen
circumstances	Sachlage, äußere Umstände, Gegebenheiten
claim	Forderung, Beanstandung
clear	klar, deutlich, verständlich
collateral	Kreditsicherheit
collection	Abholung
colloquial (language)	Umgangssprache
commence (verb)	anfangen, beginnen
communication channel	Kommunikationskanal
company delegate	Firmenvertreter
compared with	im Vergleich zu
compensation	Entschädigung, Entgelt
competitive	konkurrenzfähig
competitive strategy	Wettbewerbsstrategie
complain (verb)	sich beschweren, reklamieren
complaint	Beschwerde
complete	vollständig, komplett
complete (verb)	vervollständigen
complimentary close	Grußformel (am Briefende)
comply with (verb)	entsprechen, erfüllen
compose (verb)	zusammenstellen
concerned	betroffen, besorgt, beunruhigt
concerning	betreffend, bezüglich
concise	prägnant, knapp, komprimiert, präzise, treffend
conclusion	Schlussfolgerung, Feststellung, Abschluss
concourse	Eingangshalle, Eingangsbereich,
condition	Bedingung, Voraussetzung
conduct (verb)	führen, leiten, sich verhalten
confidentiality	Vertraulichkeit, Diskretion
confidently	zuversichtlich
confirm (verb)	bestätigen
confirmation	Bestätigung
conform to (verb)	entsprechen, übereinstimmen
conglomerate	Mischkonzern
connecting flight	Anschlussflug
consensus	Konsens, Übereinstimmung
consider (verb)	berücksichtigen, bedenken, erwägen
considerable	erheblich, beträchtlich
consignment	Sendung, Lieferung
construction and building	Bau, Bauwesen
consult (verb)	sich wenden an, zu Rate ziehen, befragen, konsultieren
consultant	Berater
consultation	Beratung, Informationsgespräch
consulting firm	Unternehmensberatung
contain (verb)	beinhalten, enthalten
content	Inhalt
continuously	ständig, ununterbrochen, (an) dauernd, stetig
contribution	Beitrag, Anteil, Zuschuss, Spende, Verdienst
convenient	angenehm, bequem, komfortabel
convention	Kongress, Tagung, Konvent
convention centre	Tagungszentrum
conversational	unterhaltend, plauderhaft
convertible	Cabriolet (Pkw)
convince (verb)	überzeugen
core skill	Kernkompetenz
corporate culture	Unternehmungskultur
corresponding	entsprechend, dazugehörig
costing	Kostenrechnung
costly	kostspielig, teuer
cover (verb)	decken, abdecken
covering note	Begleitschreiben
crate	Kiste
credible	glaubwürdig
credit	Haben (Konto)
credit (exam)	mit Erfolg bestehen
credit (verb)	(einem Konto) gutschreiben
credit exposure	Ausfallrisiko
crossed cheque	Verrechnungsscheck
crucial	entscheidend, wichtig, bedeutend
cumbersome	mühselig, unhandlich
currency	Währung

current	aktuell
current assets	Umlaufvermögen
curriculum vitae (CV)	Lebenslauf
customer	Kunde
customs	Zoll
daily	täglich
damaged	beschädigt
dated	vom (Datum); veraltet
daunting	abschreckend, einschüchternd
deadline	Frist, Abgabetermin, Stichtag, Anmeldeschluss
deal with (verb)	sich kümmern um
debit	Soll (Konto)
debit (verb)	(von einem Konto) abbuchen
debt	Schulden
decide (verb)	entscheiden
decided	entschieden
decision	Entscheidung
decision-making	Entscheidungen treffen
decisiveness	Entscheidungsfreudigkeit, Entschlossenheit
declined	abgelehnt
decrease (verb)	verringern
deduct (verb)	abziehen
delay (verb)	verzögern, verschieben
delegate	Abgesandter, Bevollmächtigter
delegation	Abordnung
delete (verb)	löschen
delivery	Lieferung
demonstrate (verb)	vorführen, zeigen, veranschaulichen
department	Abteilung
department head	Abteilungsleiter
department report	Abteilungsbericht
departure	Abflug, Abfahrt
dependable	zuverlässig
depreciation	Abschreibung
desire	Wunsch
desk	Schreibtisch
despite	trotz
details	Einzelheiten
deteriorate (verb)	sich verschlechtern, nachlassen
developed	entwickelt
development	Entwicklung
deviation	Abweichung
device	Gerät
dial a number (verb)	eine Nummer wählen
diary	Terminkalender
difference	Unterschied
different	unterschiedlich, verschieden
disadvantage	Nachteil
discipline yourself (verb)	sich diszipliniert verhalten
discount	Rabatt
discover (verb)	entdecken
dispatch	Versand
dispatch (verb)	verschicken, versenden
dispense with (verb)	überflüssig machen
disregard (verb)	ignorieren, außer Acht lassen
dissatisfaction	Unzufriedenheit
dissatisfied	unzufrieden
distance	Entfernung
distinction (exam)	mit Auszeichnung bestehen
distraction	Ablenkung
distribute the time efficiently (verb)	Zeit effizient verteilen
distributed	verteilt
divide (verb)	(auf)teilen
divisions	Abteilungen, Bereiche, Sparten
documents against acceptance (D/A)	Dokumente gegen Akzept
documents against payment (D/P)	Dokumente gegen Zahlung
done	erledigt
door opener	Türöffner
door-to-door	frei Haus
double (verb)	verdoppeln
downtime	Ausfallzeit, Stillstand, Nutzungsausfall
draft	Wechsel
draft (verb)	entwerfen
draw attention (verb)	Aufmerksamkeit auf etwas lenken
drawback	Nachteil
due	fällig, gebührend, ordnungsgemäß
due date	Stichtag, Termin
due to	bedingt durch, aufgrund von
duplicate	Kopie, Duplikat
economies of scale	Skaleneffekte, Größenvorteile
economies of scope	Synergie-Effekte
edge down(wards) (verb)	leicht fallen, nachgeben
edge up(wards) (verb)	leicht ansteigen, anziehen
education	Bildung, Ausbildung
effort	Mühe, Anstrengung, Bestreben
efforts	Bemühungen
elevator	Fahrstuhl
emergency	Notfall
emotional appeal	emotionaler Anreiz
employ (verb)	verwenden, einsetzen, einstellen (Personal)
employ a method (verb)	eine Methode anwenden
employee	Mitarbeiter, Angestellter
employer	Arbeitgeber
enable (verb)	ermöglichen
enclosed	beiliegend, in der Anlage
encounter (verb)	treffen
endless	endlos
engaged	besetzt (Telefon)
engagements	Termine
engineering	Maschinenbau, Ingenieurwesen
enquiry	Anfrage
ensure (verb)	sicherstellen
enterprise	Unternehmen
entertainment	Unterhaltung
environment	Umgebung, Umfeld
environmental technology	Umwelttechnologie
equal	gleich
equipment	Zubehör, Ausstattung, Ausrüstung
equity	Eigenkapital
error	Fehler
Errors and omissions excepted. (E&OE)	Irrtümer und Auslassungen vorbehalten.
especially	besonders, speziell
essential	wesentlich, notwendig, unentbehrlich
established	etabliert, anerkannt, akzeptiert
established in	gegründet im Jahre
estate	Grundstück, Industriegelände, Anwesen, Siedlung
estate (car)	Kombi (Pkw)
estimate	Kostenvoranschlag, Schätzung
even	sogar, gleichmäßig, geradzahlig
even out (verb)	sich einpendeln, ausgleichen, abschwächen
event	Veranstaltung, Ereignis
eventualities	Eventualitäten, Möglichkeiten
evidence	Nachweis, Beweis, Beleg
ex works (EXW)	ab Werk, zuzüglich Versandkosten
examination	Prüfung, Untersuchung
examined	geprüft, untersucht
example	Beispiel
except	außer
exhibition	Ausstellung
expanded	expandiert, erweitert, ergänzt
expect (verb)	erwarten
expense (at your expense)	auf Ihre Kosten
expenses	Ausgaben
experience	Erfahrung
experience (verb)	erleben, erfahren
explanation	Erklärung, Erläuterung
express (verb)	zum Ausdruck bringen
extensive	umfassend, ausführlich
facility	Einrichtung, Anlage
factor of production	Produktionsfaktor
factory	Fabrik
factual	sachlich, faktisch

fail (verb)	durchfallen, nicht bestehen, versagen
fairly	ziemlich
faithfully (Yours faithfully)	Mit freundlichen Grüßen
familiar with	vertraut mit
famous	berühmt
fashion	Mode
faulty	fehlerhaft, mangelhaft
favourable	vorteilhaft, günstig
feature	Produktmerkmal, Ausstattungsmerkmal
fee	Gebühr, Honorar
fewer	weniger
figures	Zahlen, Daten
file	Akte
filing cabinet	Aktenschrank
fill in (verb)	ausfüllen
findings	Ergebnisse, Resultate
focus (verb)	sich konzentrieren
follow up (verb)	verfolgen, weiter bearbeiten
forced (to)	gezwungen
forthcoming	kommend, künftig, bevorstehend
fortnight	zwei Wochen
forward (verb)	schicken, senden
founded	gegründet
framework	Rahmen, Raster, Struktur, System, Entwurf
free	kostenlos
free consultation	kostenlose Beratung
free delivery	kostenlose Lieferung, Lieferung frei Haus
freelancer	freier Mitarbeiter, Freiberufler
freight	Fracht
frequent	häufig
front-facing	nach vorn gerichtet
fundamental	grundlegend, wesentlich, elementar
furniture	Möbel
further to	mit Bezug auf
furthermore	außerdem, zudem, ferner, darüber hinaus
generally	im Allgemeinen, generell, gewöhnlich
generate (verb)	erzeugen, (er)schaffen
geriatric care	Altenpflege
get hold of s.o. (verb)	jmd. erreichen
get the job done (verb)	die Aufgabe erledigen
get through (verb)	durchkommen
get to the point (verb)	zur Sache kommen
get together (verb)	zusammenkommen, treffen
gift	Geschenk
give it "your own spin" (verb)	den eigenen Touch geben

goal	Ziel
goods	Waren, Güter, Artikel
gossiping	Geschwätz, Klatsch, Tratsch, Gerede
government	Regierung, Verwaltung
grab the reader's attention (verb)	die Aufmerksamkeit des Lesers gewinnen
gradual	schrittweise, allmählich
grammar	Grammatik
grant (verb)	gewähren
ground transportation	Bus- und Bahnverbindungen
guarantee	Garantie, Gewährleistung
habit	Gewohnheit, Angewohnheit
handling charges	Umladekosten, Bearbeitungsgebühren
hardcopy	Ausdruck, Kopie
hassle	Ärger, Mühe, Schwierigkeiten
hatchback	Fließheck, 5-Türer (Pkw)
haulier	Spediteur, Frachtführer
heading	Überschrift, Titel
head office	Hauptsitz, Zentrale
head up the ... department (verb)	die ... - Abteilung leiten
headline	Überschrift, Schlagzeile, Titel
headquarters	Hauptsitz, Zentrale, Hauptquartier
hesitate (verb)	zögern
highlight (verb)	hervorheben
high-volume	große Menge
hire (verb)	einstellen
hockey stick (verb)	plötzlich stark ansteigen
Hold on, please.	Bitte warten Sie.
Hold the line, please.	Bleiben Sie bitte am Apparat.
host (verb)	(als Gastgeber) veranstalten
however	jedoch
huge	riesig
human resources management	Personalmanagement
I didn't catch that.	Das habe ich nicht verstanden.
illustrate (verb)	darstellen, veranschaulichen
imagine (verb)	sich etw. vorstellen
immediate settlement	sofortige Begleichung
immediately	sofort
important	wichtig
impression	Eindruck
improve (verb)	verbessern
improved	verbessert
improvement	Verbesserung
in a matter of hours	innerhalb weniger Stunden

in addition to	zusätzlich zu
in advance	im Voraus
in charge (of)	verantwortlich (für)
in due course	zu gegebener Zeit
in excess of	mehr als
in order to	um ... zu ...
in stock	auf Lager, lieferbar, vorrätig
interpreter	Dolmetscher
in the event of	im Falle von
in the meantime	in der Zwischenzeit
in total	insgesamt
in-basket	Posteingang
incentive	Anreiz
income	Einkommen
income statement	Gewinn- und Verlustrechnung (GuV)
incomplete	unvollständig
inconvenience	Unannehmlichkeit
increase (verb)	erhöhen, steigern
indispensable	unverzichtbar
information exchange	Informationsaustausch
innovative	neuartig, innovativ
insist on (verb)	auf etw. bestehen
instant	sofort
instantly	sofort, unmittelbar, umgehend, augenblicklich
instead (of)	anstatt, stattdessen
instruction	Anweisung, Angabe, Belehrung, Schulung
insurance	Versicherung
insurance certificate	Versicherungsschein, Versicherungszertifikat
intense	stark, heftig, intensiv
interest	Interesse, Zinsen
interest rate	Zinssatz
interrupt (verb)	unterbrechen, stören
interruption	Unterbrechung, Störung
introduce (verb)	einführen
introduction	Einführung
invitation	Einladung
invoice	Rechnung
involve (verb)	einbeziehen, beinhalten, umfassen, bestehen in, beteiligen, betreffen
involvement/involving	Beteiligung
irreplaceable	unersetzlich
irresistible	unwiderstehlich
issue	Ausgabe (Zeitschrift); Angelegenheit, Sachverhalt, Problem
item	Stück, Artikel, Gegenstand
itemize (verb)	auflisten, einzeln aufführen
items	Artikel, Posten, Teile
justification	Rechtfertigung

key ...	Schlüssel.... , wichtige ....
key tasks	wichtige Aufgaben, Schlüsselaufgaben
kind	Art
kind(ly)	freundlich
knowledge	Wissen
known as	bekannt als
laboratories	Labore, Laboratorien
land line	Festnetz, -anschluss
last (verb)	dauern, andauern, reichen, sich halten
latest	aktuell
launch (verb)	auf den Markt bringen, starten
law and legal affairs	Jura und rechtliche Angelegenheiten
lead (verb)	leiten, führen
lead paragraph	erster Absatz eines Textes
leaflet	Prospekt
lease	Pacht
leave	Urlaub, Beurlaubung
legitimate	rechtmäßig, gerechtfertigt, berechtigt, legitim
length	Länge
less	weniger
letter of credit (L/C)	Akkreditiv
level off (verb)	sich einpendeln, gleich bleiben, abschwächen
liabilities	Verbindlichkeiten
likely	wahrscheinlich
limited	begrenzt, beschränkt
limited edition	limitierte Auflage, Sonderserie
listed on	(auf)gelistet, aufgeführt
listen (verb)	zuhören
loan	Darlehen, Kredit
located	gelegen, befindlich
locate (verb)	finden
location	Ort
logistics	Logistik
long-term	langfristig
look after (verb)	sich kümmern um
look forward to (verb)	sich freuen auf
look into (verb)	prüfen, untersuchen, nachgehen
loss	Verlust
machinery breakdown	Maschinenschaden, -störung, -ausfall
magazine	Zeitschrift
magnetic	magnetisch, anziehend, unwiderstehlich
main	Haupt....
main priority	höchste Priorität
mainly	hauptsächlich
maintenance	Wartung
majority	Mehrheit, Mehrzahl

make an effort (verb)	sich anstrengen, sich bemühen
make good (verb)	wiedergutmachen (Schaden)
malfunction	Fehlfunktion, Störung, Defekt
Managing Director	Geschäftsführer
mandatory	verpflichtend, vorgeschrieben
manufacturer	Hersteller
manufacturing	Herstellung, Erzeugung, Produktion
margin	Gewinnspanne
marked	merklich, deutlich
market leader	Marktführer
market research	Marktforschung
market share	Marktanteil
matter	Angelegenheit
matters arising	Status der Umsetzung der Beschlüsse der letzten Konferenz
meal	Mahlzeit, Essen
measuring	mit den Maßen
mentioned	erwähnt
midday	Mittag
minutes	Protokoll
miss (verb)	verpassen, versäumen
missing	fehlend
mistakes	Fehler
misunderstanding	Missverständnis
modified	modifiziert, verändert, angepasst
moreover	außerdem, zudem, ferner, darüber hinaus
mortgage	Hypothek, Grundschuld
moving sidewalk	rollender Gehsteig, Rollsteig
multi-user licenses	Mehrfachlizenzen
narrow	schmal, eng
native speaker	Muttersprachler
nearly	fast
necessarily	notwendigerweise
necessary	notwendig, erforderlich
need	Notwendigkeit
needed	benötigt
needs	Bedürfnisse
neglect (verb)	vernachlässigen
negligible	geringfügig, vernachlässigbar, unerheblich
negotiations	Verhandlungen
neither (nor)	weder (noch), kein(er), auch nicht
net	netto, ohne (Mehrwert-)Steuer
nevertheless	dennoch, trotzdem, nichtsdestoweniger
noisy	laut
nonstop	ununterbrochen, durchgehend, pausenlos
nose-dive (verb)	einbrechen, stark abfallen
note(s)	Notiz(en)

notice (at short notice)	Ankündigung (kurzfristig)
noticeable	auffallend, erkennbar, wahrnehmbar, merklich
nowadays	heutzutage
numerous	zahlreich, mehrfach, reichlich
nursing	Pflege, Krankenpflege
objective	Ziel
objectives	Ziele
obligation	Verpflichtung
obtain (verb)	beschaffen, beziehen, erhalten, bekommen
odd	ungerade, eigenartig, seltsam
of good standing	mit gutem Ansehen/Ruf
of utmost importance	von größter Wichtigkeit/Bedeutung
offer	Angebot
old-fashioned	altmodisch
on behalf of	im Auftrag/Namen von
on condition	unter der Bedingung
on sale	im Angebot, zum Verkauf
once again	noch einmal, nochmals
onwards (from ... o'clock onwards)	von ... Uhr an, ab ... Uhr
open plan office	Großraumbüro
operate in the field of ... (verb)	im Bereich ... tätig sein
operations	Geschäftstätigkeit
opportunity	Gelegenheit, Chance, Möglichkeit
optional	freiwillig, wahlweise
order	Auftrag
ordinary	gewöhnlich, alltäglich, normal
originally	ursprünglich
outcome	Ergebnis, Resultat
outdated	veraltet, überholt
outline	Entwurf, Skizze
outstanding	unbezahlt, ausstehend; hervorragend
overdeliver	mehr als versprochen liefern
overdue	überfällig
overlooked	übersehen
oversized	übergroß, überdimensional
PA system	Beschallungsanlage, PA-Anlage
packing	Verpackung
paid in full	vollständig bezahlt
paper jam	Papierstau
paper-based	papierbasiert, auf Papier
paperwork	Papierkram, Büroarbeit
paragraph	Absatz

participate (verb)	teilnehmen
participants	Teilnehmer
particular	besonders, bestimmt, speziell
pass an exam (verb)	eine Prüfung bestehen
pay a visit (verb)	einen Besuch abstatten
payee	Zahlungsempfänger
payment on receipt of goods	Zahlung bei Erhalt der Waren
payment on receipt of invoice	Zahlung bei Rechnungserhalt
peak	Gipfel, Spitze, Höchstwert
perform (verb)	ausüben, ausführen, leisten
period	Zeitraum
peripheral	nebensächlich, peripher
perishable	vergänglich
persuasion	Überredung, Überzeugung, Beeinflussung
persuasive	überzeugend, überredend, beeinflussend
petty	kleinlich
pharmaceutics and pharmacology	Pharmazie und Pharmakologie
pick-up service	Abholservice
place an order (verb)	eine Bestellung aufgeben
plain	einfach, schlicht
plant	Werk, Betrieb, Produktionsanlage, Fabrik
Please note	Bitte beachten Sie
plummet (verb)	plötzlich stark fallen
plunge (verb)	plötzlich stark fallen
point out (verb)	betonen, hinweisen
polite	höflich
poor	schlecht, schwach, arm
poor quality	schlechte Qualität
possibility	Möglichkeit
possible	möglich
postage	Porto, Frankierung
postal services	Postdienstleistungen
postscript	Nachschrift
potential	möglich
powerful	schlagkräftig, leistungsstark
practise (verb)	üben, ausüben, trainieren
precision	Präzision, Genauigkeit
prefer (verb)	bevorzugen
premises	Geschäftsräume
pre-paid postage	freigemacht, im Voraus bezahltes Porto
preparation	Vorbereitung
prepare (verb)	vorbereiten
present	anwesend, momentan, gegenwärtig
presently	gegenwärtig, momentan
press reception	Pressekonferenz
pressing	dringend, akut
pressure	Druck
previous	vorherige
price-list	Preisliste
printer cartridges	Druckerpatronen
prior	vorherige
prior tax	Vorsteuer
prioritising	Prioritäten setzen, Schwerpunkte setzen
privacy	Geheimhaltung, Privatsphäre
probably	wahrscheinlich
proceedings	gerichtliche
Schritte	
(to start proceedings)	unternehmen
procrastinate	aufschieben, zögern
procrastinate (verb)	auf die lange Bank schieben, aufschieben
procure	(sich) verschaffen
procurement	Einkauf, Beschaffung
productivity	Produktivität
professional training	Berufsausbildung
profit	Gewinn
profit and loss account	Gewinn- und Verlustrechnung (GuV)
promise (verb)	versprechen, zusagen
promptly	schnell, umgehend
promptness	Schnelligkeit, Pünktlichkeit
proof	Beweis, Nachweis
properly	ordnungsgemäß, richtig, ordentlich
property	Eigentum
proposal	Vorschlag
propose (verb)	beabsichtigen, vorschlagen
prospect	potentieller Kunde
prove (verb)	beweisen, sich erweisen, sich herausstellen
proven	erwiesen, nachgewiesen, erprobt, bewährt
provide (verb)	bieten, liefern, zur Verfügung stellen
provisional	provisorisch, vorläufig
publication (publishing)	Verlagswesen, Veröffentlichung
publisher	Herausgeber, Verleger
punctuality	Pünktlichkeit
punctuation	Zeichensetzung
purchasing	Einkauf
purpose	Zweck
put through (verb)	durchstellen, verbinden
quadrant	Quadrant, Bereich
quarter	Quartal, Vierteljahr, Viertel
quarterly	vierteljährlich
questionnaire	Fragebogen
quickly	schnell
quite	ziemlich, ganz, recht
quotation	Angebot, Preisangabe
quote	Angebot
quote (verb)	eine Preisangabe machen
rail consignment note	Bahnfrachtbrief
raise the prospect's interest (verb)	das Interesse des potentiellen Kundens wecken
range of products	Produktpalette, Sortiment
rapid	schnell, rasch, rasant, zügig
rate	Tarif, Preis, Kurs
rates	Gebühren, Preise
rather	ziemlich, vielmehr, eher, etwas
rather than	anstatt, anstelle von
reach (verb)	erreichen
real estate	Immobilien
reallocate (verb)	neu zuweisen, neu zuteilen
receipt	Eingang der Ware, Erhalt
receipt	Quittung, Beleg, Kassenbon
receipt of goods	Erhalt der Ware, Eingang der Ware
receivables	Forderungen (Buchhaltung)
receive (verb)	empfangen, erhalten, bekommen
received	erhalten
recipient	Empfänger
reckon (verb)	meinen, denken, schätzen
recommend (verb)	empfehlen
recommended	empfohlen
records	Aufzeichnungen, Unterlagen
recover (to)	sich erholen, retten
recruit (verb)	einstellen (Personal)
recruitment	Personalbeschaffung
refer to so./sth. (verb)	an jmdn./auf etw. verweisen, hinweisen, sich auf etw. beziehen
references	Hinweise, Empfehlungen
refreshments	Erfrischungen
refund	Rückerstattung
regular	normal, regulär, standardmäßig
regulations	Bestimmungen
relationships	Beziehungen
release (verb)	herausgeben, freigeben
reliability	Zuverlässigkeit
remain (verb)	bleiben
remaining	verbleibend
remember (verb)	erinnern

remind (verb)	jmdn. erinnern
remit (verb)	überweisen
remittance/transfer	Überweisung
remote	entfernt
rent	Miete
rental car	Mietwagen
repeat (verb)	wiederholen
repetition	Wiederholung
replace (verb)	ersetzen, austauschen
replacements	Ersatz
reply	Antwort
reply (verb)	antworten
reply card	Antwortkarte
report to (verb)	unterstellt sein, Bericht erstatten
report	Bericht
requested	erwünscht, gefordert
require (verb)	benötigen, erfordern
required	benötigt
requirements	Anforderungen, Erfordernisse
research	Forschung
resolved	beschlossen
response	Antwort, Reaktion
responsibilities	Aufgaben, Verantwortungsbereich
responsible for	verantwortlich für
restate (verb)	erneut vortragen, wieder nennen
restrooms	Toiletten
result	Ergebnis
result in (verb)	resultieren, zur Folge haben
retail	Einzelhandel
retailer	Einzelhändler
return (verb)	zurückschicken
return a call (verb)	zurückrufen
return envelope	Rückumschlag
revenue	Umsatz, Erlöse, Umsatzerlöse
review	Überprüfung, Beurteilung, Rückblick, Rezension
revise (verb)	ändern, überarbeiten, revidieren
revised	geändert, korrigiert, überarbeitet
revolve around (verb)	kreisen um, sich drehen um
reward	Belohnung
rewrite (verb)	neu schreiben, überarbeiten
right away	sofort
risk	Risiko
role	Rolle, Aufgabe
rule	Regel, Vorschrift, Gebot
run the ... department (verb)	die ... -Abteilung leiten
safe	sicher
safety	Sicherheit
salary	Gehalt
sales	Verkauf, Vertrieb, Absatz
sales force	Vertriebsmitarbeiter, (Handels-) Vertreter
sales letter	Werbebrief, Reklameschreiben, Direktwerbung
sales pitch	Verkaufstaktik, Verkaufsmasche
sales representative	(Handels-)vertreter
sales representatives	Vertriebsmitarbeiter, (Handels-) Vertreter
saloon	Limousine, Stufenheck (Pkw)
salutation	Anrede, Begrüßung (am Briefanfang)
sample	Muster, Probe, Beispiel
samples	Proben, Muster
satisfied	zufrieden
satisfy (verb)	befriedigen, erfüllen
say hello to s.o. (verb)	jmd. grüßen
scale	Ausmaß, Maßstab, Skala
schedule	Zeitplan, Terminplan, Fahrplan, Terminkalender
schedule (verb)	zeitlich planen, terminieren
seating arrangement	Sitzordnung
secondary	zweitrangig, untergeordnet, weniger wichtig
secret	Geheimnis
secretarial services	Bürodienstleistungen
security	Sicherheit
sedan	Limousine, Stufenheck (Pkw)
seek (verb)	suchen, einholen
seldom	selten
select (verb)	auswählen
selection	Auswahl, Sortiment
seller	Verkäufer
sender	Absender
serious	ernst, ernsthaft, schwerwiegend, erheblich
serious delays	gravierende Verzögerungen
set	(ein)stellen
settle (verb)	begleichen (Rechnung)
settlement	Ausgleich, Begleichung
several	einige, mehrere
severe weather	schweres Unwetter
share (verb)	teilen, teilhaben, gemeinsam haben
shelf life	maximale Lagerdauer, Haltbarkeit
shipment	Versand, Verladung
shipping and handling (S/H)	Versandkosten
shipping note	Schiffszettel
shoe shine	Schuhpflege, Schuhe putzen
shortage	Engpass, Mangel
shortly	in Kürze, bald
sight draft	Sichtwechsel
sign up for (verb)	sich zu bzw. für etw. anmelden
signature	Unterschrift
significant	erheblich, bedeutsam
sincerely (Yours sincerely)	Mit freundlichen Grüßen
single room	Einzelzimmer
skill	Fähigkeit, Fertigkeit, Kompetenz
skyrocket (verb)	sprunghaft ansteigen
slight	leicht, gering, schwach
slump (verb)	plötzlich stark fallen
smoothly	glatt, reibungslos
soar (verb)	schnell ansteigen
so far	bisher, bislang
solicitor	Anwalt, Rechtsanwalt
solution	Lösung
solve (verb)	lösen
sophisticated	anspruchsvoll, hoch entwickelt, raffiniert
spare parts	Ersatzteile
speak up (verb)	lauter sprechen
specifically	besonders, speziell
specifications	Vorgaben, Anforderungen
speech	Rede, Vortrag
spell (verb)	buchstabieren
spelling	Rechtschreibung
spreadsheet	Kalkulationstabelle
staff	Mitarbeiter, Angestellte, Personal
stage	Stufe, Phase, Bühne
stage (at this stage)	zu diesem Zeitpunkt
start proceedings (verb)	gerichtliche Schritte unternehmen
state (verb)	angeben, nennen, sagen
statement	Aussage, Äußerung, Stellungnahme
statement of account	Kontoauszug, Abrechnung
station wagon	Kombi (Pkw)
stationery	Schreibwaren
stay (verb)	bleiben
steep	steil
steering group	Steuergruppe
step	Schritt, Stufe, Maßnahme
stick to (verb)	sich halten an, bleiben bei
stock (in stock)	Vorrat (auf Lager, lieferbar, vorrätig)
Stock Exchange	Börse
stocks (while stocks last)	solange Vorrat reicht
storage	Lagerung

straightforward	geradlinig, direkt, unkompliziert, ehrlich
stroller	Kinderwagen
structure (verb)	strukturieren
subject	Thema, Betreff, Gegenstand, Fach
subject to	vorbehaltlich
subject to prior sale	Zwischenverkauf vorbehalten
submit (verb)	unterbreiten (Angebot), einreichen
submitted	eingereicht (z.B. Vorschlag, Protokoll etc.)
subsidiary	Filiale, Zweigstelle
substandard	minderwertig, Ausschuss
substantial	erheblich, beträchtlich
substituted	ersetzt, ausgetauscht, ausgewechselt
success	Erfolg
successful	erfolgreich
suggest (verb)	anregen, vorschlagen
suggested	vorgeschlagen
suitable	passend, geeignet
summarize (verb)	zusammenfassen
superior	Vorgesetzter
superior (adj.)	ausgezeichnet, überlegen
supplier	Lieferant
supply (verb)	liefern
support	Unterstützung
surge (verb)	plötzlich ansteigen
surname	Nachname
surprise	Überraschung
switched on	eingeschaltet
systematically	systematisch
take a message (verb)	eine Nachricht entgegennehmen
take advantage of (verb)	nutzen
take care of (verb)	sich kümmern um, erledigen
take five (verb)	5 Minuten Pause machen
Take five!	Machen Sie 5 Minuten Pause!
take into consideration ziehen (verb)	in Erwägung
take measures (verb)	Maßnahmen ergreifen
take place (verb)	stattfinden
tariffs	Gebühren, Preise
task	Aufgabe, Auftrag
tax	Steuer
taxation	Besteuerung, Steuern
telephone line	Telefonleitung, Anschluss, Festnetz (land line)
temporarily	vorübergehend, vorläufig, einstweilig
tend to (verb)	zu etw. tendieren, zu etw. führen
terms	Bedingungen
Terms and Conditions of Business	Geschäftsbedingungen
terms of delivery	Lieferbedingungen
terms of payment	Zahlungsbedingungen
That will do.	Das ist genug.
theme	Thema
therefore	daher, darum, deshalb
thorough	gründlich, sorgfältig, solide, umfassend
throughout the day	tagsüber
tidy up (verb)	aufräumen
tidying up	Aufräumen
tight deadlines	knappe Termine, knappe Fristen
timetable	Zeitplan, Fahrplan, Terminkalender
tired of	es leid sein, es satt haben
toll-free	gebührenfrei
topic	Thema
tourism	Tourismus
tracking	Sendungsverfolgung
trade discount	Händlerrabatt, Branchenrabatt
trade fair	(Fach-)Messe
training	Schulung
translate (verb)	übersetzen
transmit (verb)	übertragen
travel …	Reise…
travel arrangements	Reisevorbereitungen
trial	Probe, Test, Versuch
trial order	Probeauftrag
trouble	Schwierigkeiten, Ärger
troubleshooting	Fehlerbehebung
true copy	genaue Kopie, (wirklichkeits-) getreue Kopie
trust (verb)	vertrauen, sich verlassen auf, hoffen
turn out (verb)	(sich) erweisen als, herausstellen als, entwickeln
turn up for sth. (verb)	zu etw. erscheinen (z.B. Konferenz)
twice	zweifach, doppelt, zweimal
unable	nicht in der Lage
unanimous	einstimmig
unconditional	uneingeschränkt, bedingungslos, vorbehaltlos
underpromise	weniger versprechen
unequal	ungleich
unfortunately	bedauerlicherweise, leider
unique	einzigartig
unnecessary	unnötig
unsatisfactory	unbefriedigend
up to date	auf den neuesten Stand
upcoming	bevorstehend, anstehend, kommend
upon which	auf dem/der, auf welchem/welcher
urgent	dringend
usefulness	Nützlichkeit, Nutzen, Zweckmäßigkeit
useless	nutzlos, unbrauchbar, unnütz, vergeblich
usually	normalerweise
valid	gültig
valuable	wertvoll
value	Wert, Betrag
vary (verb)	abweichen, sich unterscheiden, variieren
venue	Ort, Tagungsort, Treffpunkt
vital	unerlässlich, lebenswichtig
voucher	Gutschein
wage	(Stunden-)lohn
warehouse	Lager, Lagerhaus, Depot
warehousing	Lagerung
warranty	Garantie, Gewährleistung
waste	Abfall, Verschwendung, Ausschuss
waste (verb)	verschwenden, vergeuden
We trust that	Wir hoffen, dass
wheelchair	Rollstuhl
whenever	sobald, sooft, jedes Mal wenn, wann auch immer
whereas	während, wohingegen, indes
whether	ob
while	während
while stocks last	solange Vorrat reicht
white space	Anteil an Leerraum/Freiraum in einem Schriftstück
whole	ganz
wholesaler	Großhändler
Will do.	Werde ich tun.
willing	bereit
with reference to	mit Bezug auf
with regards to	mit Bezug auf
with regret	mit Bedauern
without engagement	freibleibend, unverbindlich
without notice	ohne Ankündigung
wonder (verb)	sich etw. fragen
word perfect	fehlerlos
word processing	Textverarbeitung
workload	Pensum, Arbeitsbelastung, Arbeitsanfall
yield	Ertrag
You're welcome.	Gern geschehen.
Yours faithfully	Mit freundlichen Grüßen
Yours sincerely	Mit freundlichen Grüßen

Alphabetische Wortliste

ab Werk	ex works (EXW)
abbuchen (von einem Konto)	to debit
abdecken	to cover
Abfall	waste
Abflug, Abfahrt	departure
Abgabetermin	deadline
abgelehnt	declined
Abgesandter	delegate
abgesprochen	agreed
Abholservice	pick-up service
Abholung	collection
Abkürzung	abbreviation
Ablenkung	distraction
Abrechnung	statement of account
Absatz	sales
Absender	sender
Abteilung	department, division
Abteilung leiten	to head up/to run the ... department.
Abteilungsbericht	department report
Abteilungsleiter	department head
abweichen	to vary
abwesend	absent
Abwicklung	transaction, completion, fulfilment
abziehen	to deduct
Akkreditiv	letter of credit (L/C)
Akten	files
Aktenschrank	filing cabinet
aktuell	current, latest
akzeptieren	to accept
akzeptiert	established
allenfalls	at best, at (the) most
alltäglich	ordinary, usual, regular
Altenpflege	geriatric care
Alter	age
altmodisch	old-fashioned
an jmdn. verweisen	to refer so. to so.
andauernd	continuously
ändern	to alter, to modify, to revise
anerkannt	established
anfangen	to begin, to commence
Anforderungen	requirements, specifications
Anfrage	enquiry
angeben, nennen, sagen	to state
Angebot	offer, quote, quotation
Angelegenheit	matter, issue, case
Angelegenheiten	affairs
angenehm	convenient, comfortable
angepasst	adapted
Angestellte	staff, employees, personnel, workforce
Angewohnheit	habit

Anhang	attachment (E-Mail), enclosure (Brief)
anhängen	to attach (E-Mail), to enclose (Brief)
ankündigen	to announce
Ankunft	arrival
Anlage	enclosure (Brief), attachment (E-Mail)
Anlage	facility
anlocken	to attract
Anmeldeschluss	deadline
Annahme (eines Angebots/Vorschlag)	acceptance
annehmen	to accept
Anpassung	adjustment
Anrede	salutation
anregen	to encourage
Anrufbeantworter	answering machine
Anschlussflug	connecting flight
ansprechen (eines Sachverhalts/Problems)	to address
anspruchsvoll	sophisticated, demanding
anstatt	rather than, instead of
anstehend	upcoming
Anstrengung	effort
Anteil	share, part
Antwort	response, reply, answer
antworten	to reply
Antwortkarte	reply card
Anwalt	solicitor, lawyer
Anweisung	instruction, order
anwenden	to apply
Anwendung	application, app
anwesend	present
Anwesender	attendee
Anwesenheit	attendance
Arbeitgeber	employer
Arbeitsbelastung	workload
Archivierung	archival storage
Ärger	hassle, trouble
Artikel	item, article
auf den Markt bringen	to launch
auf den neuesten Stand	up to date
auf etw. bestehen	to insist on
auf etw. verweisen	to refer to sth.
auf Lager	in stock, available
auf Papier	paper-based
Aufgabe	assignment, task, role
Aufgabe erledigen	to get the job done
Aufgabenbereich	responsibilities
aufgrund von	due to
auflisten	to itemize, to list
Aufmerksamkeit	attention
aufnehmen	to accommodate
aufräumen	to tidy up
aufschieben	to procrastinate
aufteilen	to divide

Auftrag	task, assignment, order
auftreten	to arise, to appear, to happen
Aufzeichnung	record
augenblicklich	immediate(ly), instant(ly)
Ausbildung	education, (professional) training
Ausdruck	print-out, hardcopy
Ausfall	breakdown
Ausfallzeit	downtime
ausführen	to perform, to carry out
ausführlich	extensive
ausfüllen	to fill in
Ausgabe (Zeitschrift)	issue
ausgezeichnet	excellent, outstanding, superior
Ausgleich (Rechnung, Konto)	settlement
Ausmaß	scale
Ausrüstung	equipment
Aussage	statement
Ausschuss	waste
außer	except
außer Acht lassen	to disregard
außerdem	furthermore, moreover
Äußerung	statement
ausstatten (mit)	to equip (with)
Ausstattung	equipment
Ausstattungsmerkmal	feature
ausstehend	outstanding
Ausstellung	exhibition
austauschen	to replace
ausüben	to perform
Auswahl	selection, choice
auswählen	to select
Auszeichnungen	awards
Automobiltechnologie	automotive technology
Bahnfrachtbrief	rail consignment note
basieren auf	to be based on
Bau, Bauwesen	construction and building
Bausteine	building blocks
beabsichtigen	to intend
Beanstandung	claim
Bearbeitungsgebühren	handling charges
bedauerlicherweise	unfortunately
bedenken	to consider
bedeutend	crucial
Bedienungsanleitung	instructions, manual, user guide
bedingt durch	due to
Bedingungen	terms, condition
Bedürfnisse	needs
Beeinflussung	persuasion
befindlich	based in, located in
befriedigen	to satisfy

beginnen	to begin, to commence
begleichen (Rechnung)	to settle
Begleichung (Rechnung)	settlement
Begleitschreiben	covering note
begrenzt	limited
beiliegend	enclosed
beinhalten	to contain
Beispiel	example
Beitrag	contribution
bekannt geben	to announce
Bekleidung	apparel, clothing
bekommen	to obtain, to receive, to get
Beleg	receipt
Bemühungen	efforts
benötigen	to require
benötigt	required, needed, necessary
bequem	convenient, comfortable
Berater	consultant
Beratung	consultation
berechtigt	legitimate
Bereich	area, division
Bereiche	areas
bereit	willing
bereits	already
Bericht	report
Bericht erstatten	to report to
berichtigt	amended, altered, modified, revised
berücksichtigen	to consider
Berufsausbildung	professional training
berühmt	famous
beschädigt	damaged
Beschallungsanlage	PA system
beschlossen	resolved
beschränkt	limited
Beschwerde	complaint
besetzt	engaged
besonders	especially, specific(ally), particular(ly)
besorgt	concerned
bestätigen	to acknowledge, to confirm
Bestätigung	acknowledgement, confirmation
bestellen	to order, to place an order
Bestellung aufgeben	to place an order
Besteuerung, Steuern	taxation
bestimmt	especially, specific(ally), particular(ly)
Bestimmungen	regulations
Besucher	visitor, attendee
Beteiligung	involvement
betonen	to point out, to highlight
Betrag	amount
Betreff	subject
betreffend	concerning, regarding
Betrieb	plant
Betriebsstörung	breakdown

beunruhigt	concerned
Beurteilung	review, assessment
Bevollmächtigter	delegate
bevorstehend	upcoming
bevorzugen	to prefer
bewährt	proven
Beweis	proof
beweisen	to prove
Bewerber	applicant
Bewusstsein	awareness
Beziehung	relationship
bezüglich	concerning, regarding
bieten	to provide, to offer
Bildschirm	display, screen
Bildung	education
Billigung	approval
bisher, bislang	so far
Bitte beachten Sie	Please note
Bitte warten Sie.	Hold on, please.
bleiben	to remain, to stay
Bleiben Sie bitte am Apparat.	Hold the line, please.
Blumenstrauß	bouquet of flowers
Börse	Stock Exchange
Branchenrabatt	trade discount
Broschüre	brochure
Buchführung, Buchhaltung	accounting, bookkeeping
buchstabieren	to spell
Bühne	stage
Büroarbeit	paperwork
Bürodienstleistungen	secretarial services
Bürostuhl	office chair
Bus- und Bahnverbindungen	ground transportation
Cabriolet (Pkw)	convertible
Chance	chance, opportunity
Chemie	chemistry
daher	therefore
Darlehen	loan
darüber hinaus	furthermore, moreover
darum	therefore
dauern	to last
dauernd	continuously
decken	to cover
Defekt	malfunction, fault, failure
dennoch	nevertheless
Depot	warehouse
deshalb	therefore
deutlich	articulate, clear
Direktwerbung	sales letter
Diskretion	confidentiality
Dokumente gegen Akzept	documents against acceptance (D/A)
Dokumente gegen Zahlung	documents against payment (D/P)
doppelt	twice
Drehstuhl	swivel chair
dringend	urgent, pressing
Druck	pressure, print(ing)
Druckerpatronen	printer cartridges
Duplikat	duplicate, copy

durchfallen	to fail
durchgehend	continuously, constantly, nonstop
durchkommen	to get through
durchstellen	to put through, to connect
Durchwahl	(phone) extension
eigenartig	odd
Eigenschaften	characteristics, properties
eigentlich	actually
Eigentum	property
Eigentümer	owners
Eindruck	impression
eine Vielzahl an	a variety of
einen Besuch abstatten	to pay a visit
einfach	plain, basic, fundamental, simple
einführen	to introduce
Einführung	introduction
Einführungsangebot	introductory offer, inaugural offer
Einführungspreis	introductory price, inaugural price
Eingang	entrance
Eingang der Ware	receipt of goods
Eingangsbereich, Eingangshalle	concourse, entrance hall, lobby, foyer, reception
eingereicht (z.B. Vorschlag, Protokoll etc.)	submitted
eingeschaltet	switched on
eingestellt	adjusted
einige	several
Einkaufs-	purchasing ...
Einladung	invitation
Einrichtungen	facilities
einstellen	to adjust, to set
einstellen (Personal)	to recruit, to employ, to hire
einstimmig	unanimous
einstweilig	temporarily
Einverständnis	agreement
Einzelhandel	retail
Einzelhändler	retailer
Einzelheiten	details
einzeln aufführen	to itemize
Einzelzimmer	single room
einzigartig	unique
elementar	basic, fundamental, simple
empfangen	to receive
Empfänger	recipient
empfehlen	to recommend, to advise
Empfehlung	recommendation
empfohlen	recommended, advised
endlos	endless
eng	narrow
Engpass	shortage
entdecken	to discover
entfernt	remote
Entfernung	distance
enthalten	to contain
Enthaltungen	abstentions

entscheiden	to decide
entscheidend	crucial
Entscheidungen	decisions
Entscheidungsfreudigkeit, Entschlossenheit	decisiveness
entschieden	decided
Entschuldigungen	apologies
entsprechen	to comply with, to conform to
entsprechend	according to
entwerfen	to draft
entwickeln	to develop
Entwicklung	development
Entwurf	outline, draft
Erdgeschoss	ground floor (Brit.), first floor (Amer.), bottom floor (Amer.)
Ereignis	event
Erfahrung	experience
Erfolg	success
erfolgreich	successful
erforderlich	necessary
erfordern	to require
Erfordernisse	requirements
Erfrischungen	refreshments
erfüllen	to fulfil, to satisfy, to comply with, to conform to
ergänzt	amended
Ergebnis	outcome, result
ergonomisch	ergonomic
Erhalt	receipt
Erhalt der Ware	receipt of goods
erhalten	to obtain, to receive, to get
erhältlich	available
erheblich	serious, severe
erhöhen	to increase, to raise
erinnern (jmd. an etw. erinnern)	to remind
erinnern (sich erinnern)	to remember
Erklärung	explanation
erlauben	to allow
Erläuterung	explanation
erleben	to experience
erledigt	done
Erlöse	(sales) revenue
ermitteln	to ascertain, to determine, to find out, to establish
ermöglichen	to enable
ermutigen	to encourage
ernst(haft)	serious
erprobt	proven
erreichen	to reach
erreicht	achieved
Ersatz	replacement(s)
erscheinen	to appear
ersetzen	to replace
erwägen	to consider
erwähnen	to mention
erwarten	to expect
erwiesen	proven
erwünscht	requested
Erzeugung	manufacturing, production

etabliert	established
etw. leid sein, etw. satt haben	to be tired of
etw. zu schätzen wissen	to appreciate
Eventualitäten	eventualities
Fabrik	factory, plant
Fachmesse	trade fair
Fähigkeiten	skill, ability
Fahrplan	timetable, schedule
Fahrstuhl	elevator
Fall	case
fällig	due
Fassungsvermögen	capacity
fast	almost, nearly
fehlend	missing
Fehler	error, mistake
Fehlerbehebung	troubleshooting
fehlerhaft	faulty, defective
Fehlfunktion	malfunction, fault, failure
ferner	furthermore, moreover
Fertigkeit	skill, ability
Fertigung	manufacturing, production
Festnetz, -anschluss	land line
feststellen	to ascertain, to determine, to find out, to establish
Feststellung	conclusion
Filiale	branch, subsidiary
Firma	firm, company, business
Firmengelände	premises
Firmenvertreter	company delegate
Fließheck, 5-Türer (Pkw)	hatchback
fördern	to boost, to increase, to enhance
Forderung	claim
Forschung	research
fortschrittlich	advanced
Fracht	freight
Frachtführer	haulier
Frankierung	postage
freibleibend	without engagement
frei Haus	door-to-door
freigeben	to release
freigemacht	pre-paid postage
freiwillig, wahlweise	optional
freundlich	kind
Frist	deadline
führen	to conduct
ganz	whole
Garantie	guarantee, warranty
geändert	amended, altered, modified, revised
Gebiete	areas
Gebühren	charges, rates, tariffs, fees
gebührenfrei	toll-free
geeignet	appropriate, suitable
gefordert	requested

gegen Nachnahme	cash on delivery
gegenwärtig	presently, currently, momentarily
gegründet	established, founded
Gehäuse	case, casing
Geheimhaltung	privacy
Geheimnis	secret
Geldautomat	ATM (automated teller machine)
gelegen	located
Gelegenheit	chance, opportunity
gemäß	according to
Genauigkeit	precision
Genehmigung	permission, approval
generell	generally
genügend	ample, enough
Gepäckausgabe	baggage claim
Gepäckwagen	baggage carts
Gerät	device
gerechtfertigt	legitimate
gerichtliche Schritte unternehmen	to start proceedings
Gern geschehen.	You're welcome.
Geschäftsabwicklung	business transaction
Geschäftsbedingungen	Terms and Conditions of Business
Geschäftsführer	Managing Director
Geschäftspartner	business associate
Geschäftsräume	premises
Geschäftstätigkeit	operations
Geschäftswelt	business world
Geschenk	gift, present
gestatten	to allow
Getränk	beverage
gewähren	to grant
Gewährleistung	guarantee, warranty
Gewinn	profit
Gewohnheit	habit
gewöhnlich	ordinary, usual, regular
glatt	smooth(ly)
glaubwürdig	credible
gleich	equal, alike, identical
Großauftrag	bulk order, volume order
Großhändler	wholesaler
Großraumbüro	open plan office
gründen	to found, to establish
grundlegend	basic, fundamental, simple
gründlich	thorough
Grundstück	estate
gültig	valid
Güter	goods, articles, items, products, merchandise
gutschreiben (einem Konto)	to credit
Haben (Konto)	credit
Handbuch	manual, handbook, guide

Handelsvertreter	sales representative
Händlerrabatt	trade discount
Handlung	action
häufig	frequent
Haupt....	main
Hauptquartier	headquarters
hauptsächlich	mainly
Hauptsitz	head office
herausfinden	to ascertain, to determine, to find out, to establish
herausgeben	to release
Herausgeber	publisher
Hersteller	manufacturer
Herstellung	manufacturing, production
hervorheben	to highlight
heutzutage	nowadays
Hinweis	reference
hinzufügen	to add, to attach (E-Mail), to enclose (Brief)
höflich	polite
ignorieren	to disregard
im Allgemeinen	generally
im Angebot	on sale
im Auftrag von	on behalf of
im Falle von	in the event of, in case of
im Namen von	on behalf of
im Vergleich zu	compared with, in comparison with
im Voraus	in advance, ahead
Immobilien	real estate
in der Zwischenzeit	in the meantime
in Erwägung ziehen	to take into consideration
in Kürze, bald	shortly
Industrie- und Handelskammer	chamber of commerce and industry
Industriegelände	(industrial) estate
Informationsaustausch	information exchange
informieren, mitteilen	to inform, to advise about/of
Ingenieurwesen	engineering
Inhaber	business owners
Inhalt	content
innerhalb weniger Stunden	in a matter of hours
insgesamt	in total
Interesse	interest
Irrtümer und Auslassungen vorbehalten.	Errors and omissions Excepted. (E&OE)
Jahrhundert	century
jedoch	however
jmd. an etw. erinnern	to remind so. of s.th.
jmd. erreichen	to get hold of s.o.
jmd. grüßen	to say hello to s.o.
Kabel	cable
Kalkulationstabelle	spreadsheet
Kapazität	capacity
Kassenbon	receipt

Katalog	catalogue
Kategorie	category
Kernkompetenz	core skill
Kinderbetreuung	child care
Kinderwagen	stroller
Kiste	crate, case, box
klar	clear
klären, klarstellen	to clarify
kleinlich	petty
Kombi (Pkw)	estate, station wagon
komfortabel	convenient, comfortable
Kommunikationskanal	communication channel
Kompetenz	skill, ability
Kongress	convention
konkurrenzfähig	competitive
Konnossement	bill of lading (B/L)
Konsens	consensus
Kontakt aufnehmen	to contact, to get in touch with, to approach
Konto	account
Kontoauszug	statement of account
Kopie	duplicate, copy
kostenlos	free
kostenlose Lieferung, Lieferung frei Haus	free delivery
Kostenrechnung	costing
Kostenvoranschlag, Schätzung	estimate
kostspielig, teuer	costly
Krankenpflege	nursing
Kredit	loan
Kunde	customer
Kunden	customers
kurz	brief
kurzfristig	at short notice
Labor	laboratory, lab
Ladeschein	bill of lading (B/L)
Lager	warehouse
Lagerung	storage, warehousing
Landwirtschaft	agriculture
Länge	length
langfristig	long-term
lässig	casual
laut	noisy
lauter sprechen	to speak up
Lebenslauf	curriculum vitae (CV)
leger	casual
leider	unfortunately
leisten	to perform
leistungsstark	powerful
leiten	to conduct
Lieferant	supplier
lieferbar	in stock, available
Lieferbarkeit	availability
Lieferbedingungen	terms of delivery
liefern	to provide, to supply, to deliver
Lieferung (Objekt/Transportgut)	consignment

Lieferung (Prozess/Tätigkeit)	delivery
Limousine	saloon, sedan
Logistik	logistics
löschen	to delete
lösen	to solve
Lösung	solution
Luftfahrt	aviation
Luftfrachtbrief	air waybill
Mangel	shortage
mangelhaft	faulty, defective
Marktanteil	market share
Marktforschung	market research
Marktführer	market leaders
Maschinenausfall, Maschinenschaden, Maschinenstörung	machinery breakdown
Maschinenbau	engineering
Maße (mit den Maßen)	dimensions (measuring)
Maßnahmen	measures
Maßnahmen ergreifen	to take measures
Maßstab	scale
mehr als	more than, in excess of
mehrere	several
mehrfach	multiple, numerous
Mehrfachlizenzen	multi-user licenses
Mehrheit, Mehrzahl	majority
Messe	trade fair
Methode anwenden	to employ a method
Mietwagen	rental car
minderwertig	substandard
Missverständnis	misunderstanding
mit Bedauern	with regret
mit Bezug auf	according/further to, with reference/regards to
Mit freundlichen Grüßen	Yours faithfully, Yours sincerely, Best regards
mit Sitz in	based in, located in
Mitarbeiter	staff, employees, personnel, workforce
Mittag	midday
Mittagspause	lunch break
mitteilen	to announce
Möbel	furniture
Mode	fashion
modifiziert	modified, altered
möglich	possible
Möglichkeit	possibility
momentan	presently, currently, momentarily
Mühe	effort, hassle
mühselig	awkward, cumbersome
Muster (Design)	pattern
Muster (Warenprobe)	sample
Muttersprachler	native speaker
Nachfolgemodell	successor, succeeding model, follow-up model

Nachnahme (Zahlung)	cash on delivery
Nachname	surname
Nachricht entgegennehmen	to take a message
Nachteil	drawback, disadvantage
Nachweis	proof
netto	net
neuartig	innovative
nicht bestehen	to fail
nichtsdestoweniger	nevertheless
noch einmal	again, once again
nochmals	once again
normal	ordinary, usual, regular
normalerweise	usually
Notfall	emergency
Notiz(en)	note(s)
notwendig	necessary, crucial, vital, essential
notwendigerweise	necessarily
Notwendigkeit	need
Nummer wählen	to dial a number
nutzen	to use, to utilize, to take advantage of
Nutzen	benefits, usefulness, utility
nutzlos	useless
Nutzungsausfall	downtime
ob	whether
ohne Mehrwertsteuer	excluding VAT (value added tax)
ordentlich, ordnungsgemäß	properly
Ort	venue, location, place
papierbasiert	paper-based
Papierkram	paperwork
Papierstau	paper jam
Parkhaus	car park, parking deck, parking garage
Parkplätze	parking
passend	appropriate, suitable
pausenlos	continuously, constantly, nonstop
Pensum	workload
Personal	staff, employees, personnel, workforce
Personalbeschaffung	recruitment
Personalmanagement	human resources management
Pflege	nursing
Pharmazie und Pharmakologie	pharmaceutics and pharmacology
Phase	stage
Porto	postage
Postdienstleistungen	postal services
Posteingang	in-basket
Posten	item
potentieller Kunde	prospect
prägnant	concise
präzise	concise, precise
Präzision	precision
Preis	rate
Preisangabe	quotation, quote
Preisangabe machen	to quote
Preisangebot	quotation, quote
Preise	charges, rates, tariffs, prices
Preis-Leistungs-Verhältnis	value for money
Preisliste	price-list
Preisverleihung	awards
Pressekonferenz	press reception
Privatsphäre	privacy
Probe	trial
Probe (Ware)	sample
Probeauftrag	trial order
Problem	problem, issue
Produktion	manufacturing, production
Produktionsanlage	plant
Produktionsfaktor	factor of production
Produktivität	productivity
Produktmerkmale	features
Produktpalette	range of products
profitieren	to benefit from
Prospekt	leaflet
Protokoll	minutes
provisorisch	provisional
prüfen	to examine, to look into
Prüfung	examination
Prüfung bestehen	to pass an exam
Pünktlichkeit	punctuality
Qualität	quality
Quartal	quarter
Quittung	receipt
Rabatt	discount
raffiniert	sophisticated
Rahmen	frame, framework
rasch	fast, quick, rapid, prompt, swift
Rat	advice
Reaktion	reaction, response
Rechnung	invoice
Rechnungswesen	accounting
Rechtfertigung	justification
rechtmäßig	legitimate
Rechtsanwalt	solicitor, lawyer
Rechtschreibung	spelling
Rede	speech
Regal (Plural: Regale)	shelf (plural: shelves)
Regalsystem	shelving system, shelving solution
Regel	rule
Regierung	government
regulär	ordinary, usual, regular
reibungslos	smooth(ly)
reichen	to last
reichlich	ample, numerous
reisen	to travel
Reisevorbereitungen	travel arrangements
Reklameschreiben	sales letter
reklamieren	to complain
Resultat	outcome, result
resultieren	to result in
Rezension	review
richtig	properly
riesig	huge
Risiko	risk
Rolle	role
Rollstuhl	wheelchair
Rubrik	category
Rückantwortkarte	business reply card
Rückblick	review
Rückerstattung	refund
Rückumschlag	return envelope
Sachverhalt	matter, issue
Saldo	balance
schade („Das ist schade!")	"That's a pity!", "What a pity!"
schätzen (Wert, Betrag etc.)	to estimate
schätzungsweise	approximately
schicken	to forward, to send, to ship
Schiffszettel	shipping note
schlagkräftig	powerful
Schlagzeile	headline
schlecht	poor, bad
schlicht	plain, basic
Schlüssel	key
Schlussfolgerung	conclusion
schmal	narrow
schnell	fast, quick, rapid, prompt, swift
Schnelligkeit	promptness
schon	already
Schreibtisch	desk
Schreibwaren	stationery
Schritt	step
Schulden	debt
Schulung	training, instruction
Schwerpunkt	focus, priority
schwerwiegend	serious, severe
Schwierigkeiten	difficulties, trouble, hassle, issues, problems
Seefrachtbrief	bill of lading (B/L)
selten	seldom, rarely
Sendung	consignment
Sendungsverfolgung	tracking
sich befinden	to be located (in)
sich beschweren	to complain
sich bewusst sein	to be aware of
sich beziehen auf	to refer to
sich entschuldigen	to apologize
sich erinnern	to remember
sich erweisen	to prove
sich etw. fragen	to wonder
sich etw. vorstellen	to imagine
sich freuen auf	to look forward to
sich herausstellen	to prove
sich konzentrieren	to focus
sich kümmern um	to look after, to take care of
sich unterscheiden	to differ, to vary
sich verhalten	to conduct
sich verlassen auf	to trust

sich verschaffen	procure
sich wenden an	to consult
sicher	safe
Sicherheit	safety
sicherstellen	to ensure, to make sure
sichtbar werden	to appear
Sichtwechsel	sight draft
Sitzordnung	seating arrangement
Skala	scale
Skizze	outline, draft
Skonto	cash discount
sobald	whenever
sobald wie	as soon as
sofort	immediate(ly), instant(ly)
sogar	even
solange Vorrat reicht	while stocks last
solide	thorough
Soll (Konto)	debit
Sonstiges (Tagesordnungspunkt)	any other business
sorgfältig	thorough
Sortiment	selection, range of products
Sparte	division
spätestens	at the latest
Spediteur	haulier
Spende	contribution
sperrig	bulky
speziell	especially, specific(ally), particular(ly)
standardmäßig	ordinary, usual, regular
ständig	continuously
stark, heftig, intensiv	intense
stärken	to boost, to increase, to enhance
stattdessen	rather than, instead of
stattfinden	to take place
steigern	to boost, to increase, to raise
Stellungnahme	statement
stetig	continuously
Steuer	tax
Steuergruppe	steering group
Stichtag	deadline, due date
Stillstand	downtime
stören	to interrupt
stornieren	to cancel
Störung	malfunction, fault, failure, interruption
strukturieren	to structure
Stück	piece, part, share
Stufe	stage, step
Stufenheck (Pkw)	saloon, sedan
suchen	to seek
systematisch	systematically
Tabellenkalkulation	spreadsheet (software)
Tagesordnung	agenda
täglich	daily
tagsüber	throughout the day
Tagung	convention

Tagungsort	venue
Tagungszentrum	convention centre
Tarif	rate
Teil	item, part
teilen	to divide, to share
Teilnahme	attendance
teilnehmen	to attend
Teilnehmer	attendees, participants
Telefonleitung	telephone line
Termin	appointment
terminieren	to schedule
Terminkalender	diary, schedule
Terminplan	timetable, schedule
Test	trial
Textverarbeitung	word processing
Thema	topic, subject, theme
Titel	headline
Toiletten	restrooms
Tourismus	tourism
treffend	concise
trotz	despite, in spite of
trotzdem	nevertheless
Türöffner	door opener
üben	to practise
überarbeiten	to revise
überarbeitet	revised
überdimensional	oversized
übereinstimmen	to comply with, to conform to, to match
Übereinstimmung	consensus
überfällig	overdue
übergroß	oversized
überholt	outdated
überprüfen	to crosscheck
Überprüfung	review
Überraschung	surprise
Überschrift	headline
übersehen	to overlook
übersetzen	to translate
überweisen	to remit, to transfer
Überweisung	remittance, transfer
überzeugen	to convince
Überzeugung	persuasion
üblich	usual
um ... zu ...	in order to
umfassend	thorough, comprehensive, extensive
Umfeld	environment
Umgebung	environment
umgehend	immediate(ly), instant(ly), prompt(ly)
Umladekosten	handling charges
Umsatz, Umsatzerlöse	(sales) revenue
umständlich	awkward, cumbersome
Umwelttechnologie	environmental technology
unangekündigt	without notice
Unannehmlichkeit	inconvenience
unbefriedigend	unsatisfactory
unbezahlt	outstanding

unbrauchbar	useless
und so weiter	and so on, and the like, and so forth
unentbehrlich	crucial, vital, essential
unerlässlich	vital
unersetzlich	irreplaceable
ungefähr	approximately
ungerade	odd
ungezwungen	casual
ungleich	unequal
unmittelbar	immediate(ly), instant(ly)
unnötig	unnecessary
unnütz	useless
unter der Bedingung	on condition
unterbrechen	to interrupt
Unterbrechung	interruption
unterbreiten (Angebot)	to submit
unterbringen	to accommodate
Unterbringung	accommodation
untergeordnet	secondary
unterhalb	beneath
Unterhaltung	entertainment
Unterkunft	accommodation
Unterlagen	records
Unternehmen	company, firm, business, enterprise
Unternehmensberatung	consulting (firm)
Unterschied	difference
unterschiedlich	different
Unterschrift	signature
unterstellt sein	to report to
Unterstützung	support
untersuchen	to examine, to look into
Untersuchung	examination
ununterbrochen	continuously, constantly, nonstop
unverbindlich	without engagement
unverzichtbar	indispensable
unvollständig	incomplete
Unwetter	severe weather
unzufrieden	dissatisfied
Unzufriedenheit	dissatisfaction
ursprünglich	original(ly)
Ursprungszeugnis	certificate of origin
veraltet	outdated
verändert	modified, altered
veranschaulichen	to demonstrate
veranstalten (als Gastgeber)	to host
Veranstaltung	event
verantwortlich für	in charge of, responsible for
Verantwortungsbereich	responsibilities
verbessern	to improve, to enhance
Verbesserung	improvement
verbinden	to put through, to connect
verbleibend	remaining
verderblich	perishable
Verdienst	contribution
verdoppeln	to double
vereinbart	agreed
Vereinbarung	agreement
verfügbar	available

Verfügbarkeit	availability
vergeblich	useless
vergeuden	to waste
Verkauf	sales
Verkäufer	seller
Verkaufsmasche, Verkaufstaktik	sales pitch
Verlagswesen	publication (publishing)
Verleger	publisher
vermeiden	to avoid
vermuten	to assume
vernachlässigen	to neglect
Veröffentlichung	publication (publishing)
Verpackung	packing
verpassen	to miss
verpflichtend	mandatory
Verrechnungsscheck	crossed cheque
verringern	to decrease, to reduce
versagen	to fail
Versand	dispatch, shipment
Versandabteilung	dispatch department, shipping department, forwarding department
Versandkosten	shipping and handling (S/H)
versäumen	to miss
verschicken	to dispatch, to ship, to forward
verschieben	to delay
verschieden	different
verschwenden	to waste
Verschwendung	waste
versenden	to dispatch, to ship, to forward
Versicherung	insurance
Versicherungsschein, Versicherungszertifikat	insurance certificate
Verspätung	delay
versprechen	to promise
Versuch	trial
vertagen	to adjourn
verteilen	to distribute, to circulate
vertrauen	to trust
Vertraulichkeit	confidentiality
vertraut mit	to be familiar with
Vertreter	(sales) representative
Vertreterbesuche	advertising calls
Vertrieb	sales
Vertriebsmitarbeiter	sales representatives, sales force
vervollständigen	to complete
Verwaltung	administration
verweisen auf	to refer to
verzögern	to delay
Verzögerung	delay
Vierteljahr	quarter
vierteljährlich	quarterly
vollständig	complete
vollständig bezahlt	paid in full
voluminös	bulky
vom (Datum); veraltet	dated
von größter Wichtigkeit/ Bedeutung	of utmost importance
Voraussetzung	condition, requirement
Vorauszahlung	cash in advance
vorbehaltlich	subject to
vorbereiten	to prepare
Vorbereitung	preparation
vorführen	to demonstrate
Vorgaben	specifications
vorgeschlagen	suggested
vorgeschrieben	mandatory
Vorgesetzter	superior
vorherige	previous, prior
Vorkasse	cash in advance
vorläufig	provisional, temporary, temporarily
Vorrat	stock
vorrätig	in stock, available
Vorschlag	proposal
vorschlagen	to suggest, to propose
Vorschrift	rule
Vorsitzender	chairman
Vorstellungsgespräch	(job) interview
Vorteil	advantage
vorteilhaft	favourable
Vortrag	speech
vorübergehend	temporarily
Wahl	choice
Wahlmöglichkeiten	choices
während	while
wahrscheinlich	likely, probable, probably
Währung	currency
Waren	goods, articles, items, products, merchandise
Warenprobe	sample
Wartung	maintenance
Wechsel	bill of exchange (B/E), draft
weitentwickelt	advanced
weniger	fewer, less
Werbeanzeige	advertisement, advert, ad
Werbebrief	sales letter
Werbung	advertising
werden	to become
Werk	plant
Werktage	working days, workdays
Wert	value
wertvoll	valuable
wesentlich	crucial, vital, essential, fundamental
wichtig	important, crucial, vital, essential
Wichtigkeit	importance
wie angegeben	as stated
wie vereinbart	as agreed
wieder	again
wiedergutmachen (Schaden)	to make good
wiederholen	to repeat
Wiederholung	repetition
Wissen	knowledge
Wunsch	desire
würdigen	to appreciate
Zahlen	figures
zahlreich	numerous
Zahlung bei Auftragserteilung	cash with order
Zahlung bei Erhalt der Waren	payment on receipt of goods
Zahlung bei Lieferung	cash on delivery
Zahlung bei Rechnungserhalt	payment on receipt of invoice
Zahlungsbedingungen	terms of payment
Zeichensetzung	punctuation
zeigen	to demonstrate
zeitlich planen	to schedule
Zeitplan	timetable, schedule
Zeitraum	period
Zeitschrift	magazine
Zentrale	head office
Zertifikat	certificate
Ziel	objective, goal
ziellos	aimless
ziemlich	fairly, quite, rather
zögern	to hesitate
Zoll	customs; inch
zu diesem Zeitpunkt	at this stage
zu gegebener Zeit	in due course
zu Rate ziehen	to consult
Zubehör	equipment
zudem	furthermore, moreover
zufrieden	satisfied
Zugang, Zugriff	access
zuhören	to listen
zum Ausdruck bringen	to express
zum Verkauf	on sale
zuordnen (eine Aufgabe)	to assign
zur Folge haben	to result in
zur Sache kommen	to get to the point
zur Verfügung stellen	to provide
zurückrufen	to return a call
zurückschicken	to return
zusagen	to promise
zusammenfassen	to summarize
zusammenkommen	to get together
zusammenstellen	to compose
zusätzlich zu	in addition to
Zuschuss	contribution
Zustimmung	acceptance, approval, agreement
zuteilen	to allocate
Zutritt	access
zuverlässig	dependable, reliable
Zuverlässigkeit	reliability
zuversichtlich	confident(ly)
zuweisen (eine Aufgabe)	to assign
zuzüglich Versandkosten	ex works (EXW)
zwanglos	casual
Zweck	purpose
zweifach, zweimal	twice
Zweigstelle	branch, subsidiary
zweitrangig	secondary
Zwischenverkauf vorbehalten	subject to prior sale

Abbreviations (Abkürzungen)

AGM	annual general meeting	Jahreshauptversammlung
am	in the morning (ante meridiem)	vormittags
asap	as soon as possible	sobald wie möglich
ATM	Automated Teller Machine	Geldautomat
attn	for the attention of	zu Händen
Ave	avenue	Straße; Allee
B.A.	Bachelor of Arts	[akademischer Grad]
B.Eng.	Bachelor of Engineering	[akademischer Grad]
B.Sc.	Bachelor of Science	[akademischer Grad]
B/E	bill of exchange	Wechsel
B/L	bill of lading	Konnossement, Seefrachtbrief
BBA	Bachelor of Business Administration	[akademischer Grad]
bcc	blind carbon copy	Blindkopie an
c/o	care of	zu Händen
Cat No	catalogue number	Katalognummer
CBDO	Chief Business Development Officer	Vorstand Geschäftsentwicklung
cc	carbon copy	Kopie an (E-Mail)
CCO	Chief Communications Officer	Vorstand Kommunikation und PR
CCO	Chief Creative Officer	Kreativvorstand
CEO	Chief Executive Officer	Vorstandschef, Geschäftsführer
CFO	Chief Financial Officer	Finanzvorstand, Finanzleiter
CHRO	Chief Human Resources Officer	Personalvorstand, Personalchef
CIO	Chief Information Officer	Vorstand Informationstechnologie
CLO	Chief Legal Officer	Chef-Syndikus, Chef-Justiziar
CMO	Chief Marketing Officer	Marketingvorstand
COD	cash on delivery	per Nachnahme
COO	Chief Operating Officer	Betriebsleiter
cpm	copies per month	Kopien pro Monat
CPO	Chief Press Officer	Pressechef
CRO	Chief Risk Officer	Vorstand Risikomanagement
CTO	Chief Technology Officer	Technischer Direktor
CV	curriculum vitae	Lebenslauf
CWO	cash with order	Kasse bei Auftragserteilung
D/A	documents against acceptance	Dokumente gegen Akzept
D/P	documents against payment	Dokumente gegen Zahlung
DBA	Doctor of Business Administration	[akademischer Grad]
dept	department	Abteilung
E&OE	errors and omissions excepted	Fehler und Auslassungen vorbehalten

e.g.	for example (exempli gratia)	zum Beispiel
ea	each	jeder, jedes, jeder
EE	errors excepted	Irrtümer vorbehalten
Enc	enclosure, enclosed	Anlagen
EXW	ex works	ab Werk, zuzüglich Versandkosten
i.e.	that is (id est)	das heißt
incl	including	einschließlich
L/C	letter of credit	Akkreditiv
LL.B.	Bachelor of Laws (Legum Baccalaureus)	[akademischer Grad]
Ltd	private limited company	Gesellschaft mit beschränkter Haftung
M&A	mergers and acquisitions	Fusionen und Akquisitionen
MBA	Master of Business Administration	[akademischer Grad]
MD	Managing Director	Geschäftsführer
NB	note well (nota bene)	Bitte beachten, Hinweis
p&p	postage and packing	Porto und Verpackung
pa	per annum	pro Jahr
PA	personal assistant	persönliche/r Assistent/in, Chefsekretär/in
PA system	public address system	Beschallungsanlage, PA-Anlage
PhD	Doctor of Philosophy (philosophiae doctor)	[akademischer Grad]
plc	public limited company	Aktiengesellschaft
pm	in the afternoon (post meridiem)	nachmittags
PO Box	post office box	Postfach
pp	per procurationem	in Vollmacht, in Vertretung
ppm	pages per minute	Seiten pro Minute
PR	public relations	Öffentlichkeitsarbeit
PTO	please turn over	bitte wenden
qty	quantity	Menge
R&D	research and development	Forschung und Entwicklung (F&E)
Rd	road	Straße
ref	reference	Bezug, (Ihr/Unser) Zeichen
RSVP	réspondez s'il vous plaît	um Antwort wird gebeten
S/H	shipping an handling	Versandkosten
St	street	Straße
T&CB	terms and conditions of business	Geschäftsbedingungen
VAT	Value Added Tax	Mehrwertsteuer, Umsatzsteuer
VP	Vice President	Vizepräsident
w/	with	mit
w/o	without	ohne
XO	Executive Officer	Stellvertreter des Geschäftsführers

Irregular verbs (unregelmäßige Verben)

bear	bore	born	ertragen, gebären	leave	left	left	(zurück-/ver-)lassen
beat	beat	beaten	schlagen	lend	lent	lent	(ver)leihen
become	became	become	werden	let	let	let	lassen
begin	began	begun	anfangen	lie	lay	lain	liegen
bet	bet	bet	wetten	light	lit	lit	anzünden
bind	bound	bound	binden	lose	lost	lost	verlieren
bite	bit	bit(ten)	beißen	make	made	made	machen
bleed	bled	bled	bluten	mean	meant	meant	meinen, bedeuten
blow	blew	blown	blasen	meet	met	met	(sich) treffen
break	broke	broken	(zer)brechen	pay	paid	paid	bezahlen
bring	brought	brought	bringen	put	put	put	legen, setzen, stellen
build	built	built	bauen	read	read	read	lesen
burn	burnt	burnt	(ver)brennen	ride	rode	ridden	reiten, fahren
burst	burst	burst	platzen	ring	rang	rung	klingeln, läuten
buy	bought	bought	kaufen	rise	rose	risen	aufstehen, aufgehen
catch	caught	caught	fangen	run	ran	run	laufen, rennen
choose	chose	chosen	(aus)wählen	say	said	said	sagen
come	came	come	kommen	see	saw	seen	sehen
cost	cost	cost	kosten	seek	sought	sought	suchen
cut	cut	cut	schneiden	sell	sold	sold	verkaufen
deal	dealt	dealt	handeln (von)	send	sent	sent	senden, schicken
dig	dug	dug	graben	set	set	set	(ein)stellen
do	did	done	tun	sew	sewed	sewn	nähen
draw	drew	drawn	zeichnen, ziehen	shake	shook	shaken	schütteln
dream	dreamt	dreamt	träumen	shine	shone	shone	scheinen
drink	drank	drunk	trinken	shoot	shot	shot	schießen
drive	drove	driven	fahren	show	showed	shown	zeigen
eat	ate	eaten	essen	shut	shut	shut	schließen, zumachen
fall	fell	fallen	fallen	sing	sang	sung	singen
feed	fed	fed	füttern	sink	sank	sunk	sinken, versenken
feel	felt	felt	(sich) fühlen	sit	sat	sat	sitzen, sich setzen
find	found	found	finden	sleep	slept	slept	schlafen
flee	fled	fled	fliehen	smell	smelt	smelt	riechen
fly	flew	flown	fliegen	speak	spoke	spoken	sprechen
forbid	forbade	forbidden	verbieten	spell	spelt	spelt	buchstabieren
forget	forgot	forgotten	vergessen	spend	spent	spent	ausgeben, verbringen
forgive	forgave	forgiven	verzeihen, vergeben	stand	stood	stood	stehen
freeze	froze	frozen	(ein)frieren	steal	stole	stolen	stehlen
get	got	got (gotten)	bekommen, gelangen	stick	stuck	stuck	kleben
give	gave	given	geben	strike	struck	struck	stoßen, schlagen
go	went	gone	gehen	sweep	swept	swept	fegen
grow	grew	grown	wachsen, anbauen	swim	swam	swum	schwimmen
hang	hung	hung	(auf)hängen	swing	swung	swung	schwingen
hear	heard	heard	hören	take	took	taken	nehmen, (hin)bringen
hide	hid	hidden	(sich) verstecken	teach	taught	taught	lehren, unterrichten
hit	hit	hit	schlagen, treffen	tear	tore	torn	(zer)reißen
hold	held	held	halten	tell	told	told	erzählen, sagen
hurt	hurt	hurt	verletzen, weh tun	think	thought	thought	denken, glauben
keep	kept	kept	(be)halten	throw	threw	thrown	werfen
know	knew	known	wissen, kennen	understand	understood	understood	verstehen
lay	laid	laid	legen, decken	wake	woke	woken	wecken, aufwachen
lead	led	led	führen, leiten	wear	wore	worn	tragen (Kleidung, Brille)
lean	leant	leant	lehnen	win	won	won	gewinnen
learn	learnt	learnt	lernen	write	wrote	written	schreiben